Surviving Doomsday

Author/Publisher's Note/Disclaimer

The information and other materials (collectively "Materials") contained in this book were obtained from sources believed to be reliable and accurate. The Materials may, however, contain inaccuracies or errors. The publisher and author make no representations about the accuracy, reliability, completeness, or timeliness of the Materials or about the results to be obtained from using the Materials. Neither the author, nor the publisher, shall be liable for any loss or damage allegedly arising from any information or suggestions contained in this book, and assume no liability for any incidents or injuries resulting from the use or misuse of the Material. Neither the author, nor the publisher, is engaged in providing professional advice or services to the individual reader.

The Materials provided are for illustration and/or informational purposes only, and are not, nor are they intended to provide legal, medical, or any type of professional or life saving advice. The reader should consult with an appropriate professional regarding their individual situation. Any use of the information contained in this book shall be solely at the reader's risk.

The possession, ownership and use of firearms are governed by State and Federal laws. Readers should consult the applicable laws in their jurisdiction before buying, possessing, using or otherwise engaging in any activities involving a firearm. If the reader has any doubts as to the applicable laws where they live, they should consult legal counsel.

Comments and opinions expressed in this book represent the personal views of the individuals to whom they are attributed and are not necessarily those of the publisher or author, who make no guarantee or warranty, express or implied, regarding the reliability, accuracy, or completeness of the Materials.

Any similarity or resemblance to any real persons, living or dead, actual facts or places is purely coincidental, and not intentional.

The author is not paid to endorse any products, and receives absolutely no compensation from anyone for any of the products named in this book.

ISBN: 1-4802-7066-0
ISBN-13: 9781480270664
Library of Congress Control Number: 2012921443
CreateSpace Independent Publishing Platform,
North Charleston, SC

Surviving Doomsday

A Guide for Surviving an Urban Disaster

Richard Duarte

Contents

Dedication

This book is dedicated to those people, who when faced with death, destruction and overwhelmingly desperate situations somehow still manage to find the good in humanity, to stay positive and to overcome adversity.

Acknowledgments

My special thanks to all those very special people who have supported my every endeavor; no matter how unrealistic or impractical those endeavors may have seemed at the time.

Introduction

"Educate and inform the whole mass of the people... They are the only sure reliance for the preservation of our liberty."
-Thomas Jefferson

Why You Should Read This Book

We live in a very dangerous and unpredictable world. We are often exposed to hazardous events and circumstances. Some of these events are natural, others are manmade; but all have the potential to change our lives in a single moment; usually for the worse. Within all the uncertainty, however, we all have choices. If you are taking the time to read this book, then you are already off to a very good start - you are taking responsibility and making an effort to obtain the skills necessary for survival. While life holds no guarantees for anyone, we can often increase our chances for surviving a crisis, or public emergency, simply by having a plan, thinking ahead and by making some basic preparations. Conversely, time and again, everyday people are caught completely off-guard and find themselves at the mercy of whatever crisis has come their way. Fortunately, more and more responsible people are preparing to survive, and refusing to become victims.

In just the last twenty years, there have been numerous disasters claiming many lives and causing billions of dollars in property damage. The typical disaster aftermath includes the potential for shortages of food, water, medical supplies; and in severe circumstances even social breakdown and violence. Once the downward slide begins just about anything is possible. In this book we call such events a Worst Case Scenario (WCS). A WCS is any natural or man-made event that puts people at great risk of severe physical harm or loss of life. A WCS can often lead to disruptions of our social and economic infrastructure. Examples of a WCS include, but aren't limited to, hurricanes, storms, floods, tsunamis, earthquakes, fires, acts of terrorism, war and/or civil unrest, prolonged interruptions of the supply chain or transportation systems and public services/utilities, serious economic, social or political disruptions, cyber attacks, etc. (Familiar examples include the 2011 Japanese Tsunami, Hurricane Andrew in 1992, Hurricane Katrina in 2005, the terrorist attacks on 9/11, and the 1992 L.A. Riots – recent history contains many more such events.) Sometimes these events hit very close to home.

For many people in South Florida, 1992 was a life-changing year. In the early morning hours of August 24, 1992, Hurricane Andrew, at the time the second most powerful and destructive hurricane in U.S. history, struck South Florida. Andrew, a category five hurricane, slammed into Miami at more than 160 miles per hour destroying nearly everything in its path. Andrew's full force and fury would eventually affect the North Western Bahamas, South Central Louisiana, and South Florida. A total of 65 people lost their lives, countless others were injured, and the storm caused $26.5 billion in property damage (in 1992 dollars), most of the damage was in South Florida.

At that time, I knew absolutely nothing about disaster/crisis planning. In fact, I knew less than nothing, because what little I thought I knew was mostly all wrong. I had heard the news coverage about the approaching storm, but I made no plans for leaving the area, and I made no serious preparations to secure my house. In hindsight, my biggest mistake, besides my total lack of any planning or preparation, was that I completely underestimated the seriousness of the situation. I did not realize it at the time, but I was in denial, and I would pay a very steep price for my complacency.

Before it was all over, Andrew had completely destroyed my home. At dawn, the full extent of the destruction became apparent; my neighborhood was in complete ruins. Long before any first responders began arriving, looters, and other miscreants were already looking for targets of opportunity; very scary and very sad. For me, Andrew represented an incredibly loud wake-up call. My young family and I survived by hiding in a small closet for what seemed an eternity. The experience left me shaken, but with a strong sense of determination. I knew that things could have very easily been a whole lot worse. I alone was responsible for my family, and I had failed them miserably. By not planning or preparing, I had inadvertently exposed my loved ones to tremendous risks; there was no excuse for my failure. In the aftermath, I swore I would never again be caught unprepared. Andrew had taken almost everything from me. But it had also given me something very significant – a second chance. We were all alive and healthy, and I emerged from the pile of rubble, that was once our home, with a steadfast commitment to learn everything that I could about urban survival and disaster preparedness. My brush with death had put it all in perspective; going forward I understood that it was all on me, and always would be. It's no different today, some twenty years later.

After Andrew, I knew I had to prepare, but I had no idea where to start. In 1992, when I first began my research, few people showed any interest in urban survival planning, and sources for useful information were very limited. How would I prepare? What skills did I need to learn? What supplies did I need to buy and how would I make the most effective use of my limited survival budget?

I also knew that hurricanes weren't the only threat that I had to consider; my preparations would have to take into account, just about any urban crisis - manmade or natural. The more I thought about it the more complicated and overwhelming it all seemed. If I ever hoped to be prepared for the next crisis, I needed some serious guidance. After struggling on my own for quite some time, I still had very little to show for my efforts. If a comprehensive, practical and easy-to-understand source of information was out there, I just couldn't find it. Most of the materials I found were not well suited for the urban environment, or just weren't very practical.

After many years of research, trial and error, testing and making mistakes, I eventually organized the fundamental essentials for my urban survival plan. More importantly, these were elements that anyone could understand, and put into action. This book started as a collection of notes that I intended to organize and give to my friends and relatives; since I knew that none of them would ever bother to do any of the research themselves. These were average everyday people, who never gave the topic of survival much thought. But, without the proper guidance, most of them would be terribly unprepared for any crisis – as I once was. While I couldn't prepare for them, I wanted to make it as easy as possible for them to prepare for themselves. I put together a straightforward and easy-to-understand summary for all my friends and relatives. I knew that this would simplify the process and allow them to get started without all of the complication and confusion that I had faced some twenty years earlier.

If my friends, and relatives, just took the time to read the summaries, and to do a little planning and preparing, they would be far better off than the majority of their unprepared neighbors. Those notes, ideas, suggestions, shopping lists, and general information evolved into the book you're now reading. Somewhere along the way, it became a passion of mine; and a way for me to share what I had learned, since disasters can happen to anyone at anytime, not just people in Florida.

Contrary to popular belief, you don't need to be a survival expert to be well prepared, or to have a viable survival plan. The ideas and suggestions contained in this book are meant to help average people living in an urban/suburban area to prepare and plan for a WCS; no prior survival experience necessary.

The top three goals of this book are:

1.   To readjust your mindset, and to encourage you to take responsibility for yourself and your family.
2.   To provide you with some of the resources, information and tools you need to start making preparations at your own pace, and within your own abilities and budget.
3.   To make it as easy and painless as possible for you to get started.

Remember, reading about something and actually doing it are two entirely different things. Regrettably, too many people have the best possible intentions but never take the first step. While no plan can adequately address every possible contingency, just by having a plan and making some basic preparations you will always be far better off than someone who did nothing at all; but you need to get started.

This is a process that will take time, effort and money; but you have a major advantage - someone else has already done much of the heavy lifting for you. If you've come this far, doing nothing should not even be an option for you.

"Humanity was never meant for mediocrity. Yet many among us are now, and will forever remain, limited by their profound lack of understanding. Some people develop their minds and glimpse the wisdom of the ages. Others develop their muscles and embrace the strength, power and endurance only possible of a body that obeys the heart and mind without question. An even smaller group, look inside themselves to find the peace, compassion, humility and timeless strength of character that can only be attained through spirituality. An infinitesimally smaller minority develop the intellect, strengthen and dominate the body, and come to know the true nature of their spirit - thus finding a balance that comes as close to excellence as any mere mortal can ever hope to attain."

-Richard Duarte

1: Assessment–Where We Are, and How We Got Here

"For those who fight for it life has a flavor the sheltered will never know"

-Theodore Roosevelt

Strip away the modern-day distractions and at the most basic level people need food, water, shelter and some level of relative security to survive for any length of time. These four things are pretty basic, but when you need them, you will need them desperately. As vital as they are for sustaining life, it's amazing just how often we take these things completely for granted. One explanation may be that most of us have never really been without the basics, and our attitude reflects it. We expect food on the supermarket shelves, clean water to flow from the tap, and abundant, affordable energy to power our homes, our vehicles and our modern way-of-life. If any of this sounds familiar, it's for good reason; these expectations are commonly held across vast segments of society, with very few exceptions.

On Another level, we also expect that a 911 operator will always answer our calls and immediately send help. We expect the police to be there to protect us and our property. When we're hurt or sick, we expect emergency personnel to respond promptly and attend to our injuries. We expect that the electrical grid, the transportation systems, the utilities and every other complex component of our modern-day urban infrastructure will always be there to serve our needs. On the economic side we expect our financial and banking institutions to be secure, safe and rock solid, and our currency to be stable. We have come to expect all these things and much, much more; anything less is unacceptable to us, and we have adapted our lives, and habits, accordingly. Do you see the problem yet? To all but those who are most deeply asleep, or in complete denial, the gap between expectations and reality is painfully obvious. How did we come to expect so much?

In the beginning of the twentieth century the average person lived in a very different world. Back then life was not easy, and for most folks it was rarely comfortable, but people understood what it took to survive. The majority of the population lived in rural areas, on farms or in small communities. If someone needed water - they dug a well. When they needed food, they farmed, hunted or raised farm animals. There were no supermarkets or fast food restaurants, and most homes had no electricity. People understood that they alone were responsible for their own survival and they usually rose to the challenge, or went without; that's just the way it was.

After any local disaster/emergency, no one sat around waiting for, or even expecting any outside help; folks knew that no one would be coming to their rescue. People made a level-headed calculation of the risk(s) at hand and took whatever actions were necessary; they didn't sit around waiting for anybody else to come along and fix their problems. They had to do the *fixing* themselves, there were no other options. Today, that self-reliance has all but disappeared, and has been replaced by something much different – an expectation of entitlement. In our present time, few people accept responsibility for themselves; although that doesn't stop them from expecting others to shoulder the very burden they refuse to accept.

If one single thing defines and sets us apart from our early twentieth century ancestors, it's our reliance on others for just about all the resources we consume. From the water that comes out of the faucet, the food on our table, to the energy that powers our way-of-life; it all comes from somewhere else, and from the efforts of someone else. Many of these products/resources travel thousands of miles, over land and sea, to reach their final destination. This presents yet another potential issue since this transportation infrastructure is complicated and relies on an intricate choreography involving many different components, sometimes spread out over many different continents.

The abundance and stability that we all enjoy, and expect, is in large part made possible by an uninterrupted flow of energy from sources, many of which are, far outside of our borders. Much of this energy, in the form of fossil fuels, is imported from countries in the volatile Persian Gulf region. We all know that oil/petroleum makes the modern world possible, and that without it our way-of-life would very quickly resemble life in the Middle Ages. But many of us don't fully understand how this scenario would play out and how significantly it would impact the world we expect to see every morning when we walk out of our front door. Everything we depend on for maintaining our modern existence can somehow be traced back to oil. All the resources we consume are produced, transported, processed or somehow powered by the energy we derive from petroleum or petroleum products.

Few of us ever bother to think about what would happen the day oil production is disrupted or seriously impaired as a result of a natural disaster, political instability, war, social unrest, a financial collapse or a dozen other potential tragedies. Consider for a moment that our access to food, here in the United States, is dependent on a complicated and fragile transportation system of truck and rail traffic that relies heavily on oil. How is it that we have allowed the stability, or lack thereof, of oil producing countries, many of which are openly hostile to our government, to affect our population's access to food? But yet, there it is.

As a nation, our health, welfare and stability depends not only on these far-off countries, but also on the immensely complicated and fragile infrastructure that brings their products to our shores. The U.S. has always had virtually unlimited, and very affordable, access to vast supplies of fossil fuels from around the globe – and we have come to expect that this will always be so. What will happen the day that this situation changes? Most of us don't appreciate just how serious this risk has become, and to what extent it can threaten our very existence. Even just the thought of these things happening should scare us all, but for some strange reason it doesn't. If history is destined to repeat itself, and it usually does, we will most probably wait until the very last possible moment to even begin thinking about these problems. By then it will most likely be too late to do anything but *run for cover.*

Given all the uncertainty and the high levels of risk, you would think that most people would make at least some basic preparations for their family, some food, water, medical supplies. But, if you thought that, you would be wrong. Many people will tell you that they don't prepare because that's the government's job. They still mistakenly believe that, after any disaster, *the authorities* will quickly organize and come to their aid. If you are among the many that are expecting a prompt governmental response to reestablish law, order and the supply chain, then you have not been keeping up with current events. Think about hurricane Katrina and the many other recent situations where local, state and federal authorities were caught completely unprepared, or were just plain incompetent, to deal with the size and/or complexity of the crisis and its aftermath. In many of these instances government, and its agencies, were widely criticized for their inability to adequately respond to the needs of ordinary citizens in the aftermath of the crisis. Are these the same *authorities* that you are counting on to help you and your family after a WCS?

Now, considering all of the anticipated, and actual, budget cuts at all levels of government, you should ask yourself how will it be possible for the government to do more (improve on their record of failures) with less money? Chances are that the federal and local authorities will actually do much less in the coming years. (Officials have recently raised serious concerns over budget cuts and their ability to adequately respond in the event of a widespread disaster given their limited resources. Other government officials have suggested that all funding for federal disaster agencies be completely eliminated.)

Most of us don't like this uncomfortable reality so we look away and return to our *make-believe* lives of denial and consumption. As a society, we are constantly distracted by issues of total insignificance. The national headlines are routinely dominated by celebrity gossip and news about the fairy tale lives of people we don't know, and probably never will. Even the news has become nothing more than the sensationalism of local and national pettiness. We are so desensitized by the news cycle drama, that when something really bad does happen it's almost impossible for us to accurately and rationally process the event. When a disaster happens to someone else, in some other part of the country, or the world, the news stories seem surreal to us. We often compare these events to something we once saw in a movie, since that seems to be our only frame of reference. In our minds, it's simply some far-off occurrence that is completely unrelated to us. Often, the news of real-life disasters is pushed aside, by the *news* of what celebrity couple broke up this week.

It's important to remember that not all disasters are natural, some are very much manmade. World leaders can be just as irresponsible as the average citizen. At any given moment global leaders misman-age and sometimes directly cause huge economic, social and political problems. Any of these missteps has the potential to create global chaos. The worse things get, the more people lose confidence in their leaders, their economy and the financial markets. It's a vicious cycle, and although many folks here in the U.S. still don't understand this, or just refuse to accept it, everything that happens *over there* (outside our borders) has repercussions over here (inside the U.S.).

Whether it's a natural disaster, a terrorist attack, an economic meltdown, or a pandemic – it can affect you profoundly and you need to be prepared. If a WCS were to occur, would you be ready, or would you be just another name on the long list of victims? Fortunately, the choice is yours.

2: Urban Survival–What it is, and Why You Should Care

The nice thing about failing to plan is that failure comes as a complete surprise and is not preceded by long periods of worry or concern.

- Unknown Author

In This Chapter:

- The main goal of Urban Survival Preparation/Planning is to increase your chances of staying alive, in an urban environment, during and after a WCS.
- Urban survival requires skills, supplies and preparations that are unique to the urban/suburban environment.
- After a WCS social order can deteriorate or completely break down. Panic, confusion and general frustration can drive many people to commit acts of aggression and violence; having a plan and being prepared allows you to either leave safely to a pre-determined location, or to quietly shelter in place avoiding the potential chaos outside your doors.
- No plan is ever 100%. But even some very basic preparations can dramatically increase your chances for survival. The cost of not preparing is just too high.
- Plan ahead, remain flexible and adapt to changes in circumstances.
- Hope for the best, but always be prepared for the worst. (In Survival situations what can go wrong, will go wrong.) Betting with your life should never be an acceptable gamble.

This is not a book about wilderness survival, or living off the land; although these skills can indeed be very useful and should never be neglected. I always encourage people to learn wilderness survival skills – but that, is not this.

This book is about learning the skills, and making the necessary preparations to survive in an urban/suburban environment during and after a major disaster or WCS. Plain and simple, it's about staying alive where most of us live, work and play, when everything and everybody around us is falling apart. No easy feat when you consider the fragility of the modern urban environment. With few exceptions, every major city depends entirely on electricity, fossil fuels and rural land and farmers for their food supply. Without electricity and fuel, the daily deliveries of food and other major necessities to most cities would very quickly come to an abrupt halt. Most major metropolitan areas would immediately become literal *death-traps* with millions of hungry people, and few resources to feed them.

Most, if not all, cities can't produce food in sufficient quantities to feed their own population. Most cities don't have an abundant supply of clean drinking water that doesn't come from somewhere outside of the city limits. Most, if not all, cities don't have sufficient emergency and law enforcement resources to adequately address a large scale public emergency, and a population in a state of panic after a WCS. Surprised? You shouldn't be.

We should all be "Prepared." But, what does *being prepared* mean in an urban environment? And in preparing, how can we be sure that we are utilizing our limited resources in the most efficient and effective way possible? This book is meant to provide you with the information that most people don't normally think about, or even consider.

Urban survival requires a different set of skills than wilderness survival. And why wouldn't it? When most people talk about urban survival they are usually referring to getting home after a stressful day at work and an equally stressful commute. Rarely does anyone actually use the term "survival" literally when referring to our large, sprawling urban centers.

Survival training and survival preparation have long been the domain of outdoor enthusiast and rugged wilderness types. To many people, the very word "survival" has become synonymous with the outdoors. Look at most survival books and you'll notice that the main focus is on building outdoor shelters, making fire, hunting and foraging for food. Most of us, however, live in urban centers (about 80% of the population). And although we may one day find ourselves lost in the woods, it is far more likely that we will experience some sort of urban survival crisis, since that is where we spend the majority of our time.

The survival challenges a person can expect to encounter in a city or suburban area have very little to do with the scenarios one would find in the wilderness. Knowing this, it makes perfect sense that urban dwellers need to plan and prepare to survive in a very different way. Urban survival planning and preparation will help you increase your ability to survive those crucial hours, days or maybe even weeks before police, firefighters, rescue workers, the National Guard and other first responders arrive. And realistically, even after help does arrive you should not expect your circumstances to improve much. Past experience has shown us that after a WCS first responders will usually be overwhelmed, undermanned and seriously lacking sufficient resources to address all the existing problems. And remember, getting to you and your neighbors may not even be an initial priority. Depending on the severity of the crisis, the officials making the strategic decisions will probably be under tremendous pressure to keep main roads clear, hospitals open, and to protect large, vulnerable infrastructure resources such as government buildings, power and utility installations, and nuclear power plants.

It's crucial to understand that during the initial period after a WCS, you will most probably only be able to count on yourself and the preparations you have made. True help might not arrive for weeks, maybe even months. At minimum, you should plan to have adequate supplies of food, water, and medical supplies to provide for yourself and for your group, for a minimum of three months. Being prepared will bring you comfort and a certain peace of mind, knowing that at least you have secured the basics for sustaining life.

Unfortunately, being prepared may also make you a target, since there will be many people who did not prepare. The unprepared masses will see your supplies as an opportunity to obtain what they need, and can't otherwise get. Once you are discovered, they may stop at nothing to take what you have. Because of this, and many other reasons, you should also be prepared to protect yourself, and your loved ones, from the potential violence that can follow any WCS. This is nothing new we have all seen it happen many times before.

In 2005 Hurricane Katrina made landfall onto the Louisiana coast. Residents who were unprepared, and had no plan, retreated to the "shelter of last resort" the Louisiana Superdome. During the ordeal the stadium sheltered about 20,000 people who endured many days without adequate food, water or security. Despite the planned use of the Superdome as an evacuation center, it was widely reported that local, state and federal authorities all failed miserably for their lack of planning and/or preparation. The site had no water purification equipment, no chemical toilets, no medical supplies, no emergency food supplies and lacked adequate security. Residents who evacuated to the Superdome were advised to bring their own supplies – a case of *too little, too late*. Most of the evacuees either had no supplies to bring, or simply expected authorities to take care of those details for them. With no power, no clean water and only very limited supplies of food and water, eventually brought in by the Louisiana National Guard, conditions quickly deteriorated. (Does this sound like the kind of place you want to take your family to ride out a WCS or the aftermath?)

Surprisingly, the Superdome had been used twice before as a crisis shelter, in 1998 during Hurricane Georges, and in 2004 during Hurricane Ivan. You would think that the *authorities* would have had the crisis management plan *down to a science* by the time Katrina came along in 2005, but sadly that was not the case.

The Superdome fiasco is a case study on how quickly things can go wrong, and some would say, the perfect example of why none of us should ever expect the *authorities* to take responsibility for us. If there was ever a reason to prepare and to have a plan, this is it. In all fairness, this same thing could have potentially happened in any major American city. But that begs the question, where will the next *Superdome* style fiasco be?

In the aftermath of any major disaster there will always be two groups of people – the *prepared,* and the *unprepared*. After a few days without food, water, medical attention, or any vital public services, the world around you will begin to look dramatically different than anything you could ever have imagined. At best, the unprepared will wander the streets looking for help (food, water, medicine); at worst, driven by panic and desperation, normal everyday people will transform into unlawful mobs willing to do anything they can to get what they need. (Think looting, break-ins, home invasions, and an overall increase in violence, and violent crimes.)

After a WCS you can also expect dramatic increases in the activities of criminals, who by their very nature, will be inclined to prey on the weak, much as they do today, but in the absence of law and order, to a much greater and more violent degree. Think of the widespread looting, arson and murder that occurred during the 1992 Los Angeles Riots. Six days of total chaos resulted in over one billion dollars in property damage, 53 people dead, and as many as 2000 people injured. It took a dawn-to-dusk curfew, deployment of the National Guard, and U.S. Army soldiers and Marines to finally restore order.

Under the right conditions every American city has the potential to very quickly turn into a war zone. During the L.A. riots people were shooting at each other on the streets with handguns, shotguns, and semi-automatic weapons – sometimes just because they could. Under the right circumstances, that *thin veneer* that we commonly refer to as *social order* could very easily collapse. Remember that social order is a very fragile state of mind that traditionally disintegrates immediately after a disaster, or sometimes even after a sporting event that didn't turn out the way certain fans wanted. It doesn't always take an actual collapse of the electrical grid or the supply chain to incite the *masses* into total pandemonium.

For those of you who live in an area affected by the yearly hurricane season, you are familiar with the chaotic buying frenzy that occurs at your local grocery stores just before an approaching storm. It doesn't take much to throw people into a panic. Irrational, violent behavior can very easily become the norm, even among otherwise peaceful, law-abiding people.

Think of the hordes of shoppers who invade the big box retailers every year on *Black Friday*. These folks routinely trample each other to get that all-important video game, or that *special* laptop computer that's on sale. You should keep in mind, that those crazed *Black Friday* shoppers, are well fed, well-hydrated and well-rested. Imagine those very same people after a major crisis when they have not had anything to eat or drink, and maybe haven't slept for days. Now think about the criminals that routinely break the law, and consider how they will act once they realize that there is no one to stop them. These are the very same people you will have to deal with if you are unprepared, and forced to take to the streets to look for food and water.

The unprepared, desperate masses will not stop for one moment to consider their actions, when the last grocery store shelf is empty. (Shortly after the Hurricane Katrina moved away, some residents of New Orleans began looting stores, many in search of food and water, but others in search of anything they could carry away.) You should anticipate that after a disaster store shelves will be empty, utilities and public services will be disrupted or completely absent and 911 assistance may be severely delayed or entirely unavailable —this reality should not surprise anyone, but yet, for some odd reason, it always does.

The flip side of all this bad news is that for the prepared, the odds dramatically improve in their favor. Even just a little preparation and some planning will provide a major advantage. The amount of time, money, planning and overall preparation you devote to your survival plan will, in many ways, determine the ultimate success of the plan for you and your family. The only certainty in uncertain times is that there exist tremendous potential for many things to go wrong, sometimes with little or no warning. It's often not a matter of if, but only of <u>when</u> and <u>how</u>.

As a society, we have grown to expect much and to take just about everything we have for granted. Most of us live content in the hope that nothing bad will ever happen, and if it does, that someone else will need to deal with it. Don't allow yourself to get caught in this trap. The responsibility is yours and yours alone. Survival situations are always scary, full of stress and anxiety, and nothing is ever likely to turn out the way you anticipated. You can expect that even the best survival plan will be seriously challenged within the first 24 hours. But that should never stop anyone from making a thoughtful and concerted effort well in advance of any disaster.

A successful urban survival plan and basic preparations must contain and effectively address the following basic elements:

- **Water**
- **Food**
- **First Aid/Medical**
- **Personal Security/Self-Defense**
- **Leaving, Staying Put & Getting Home**
- **Hygiene/Sanitation**

The chapters that follow will deal with each of these topics, one at a time. Towards the end of this book we provide an extensive *shopping* list of core survival items, for you to consider as you begin your preparations. But remember, this is just a starting point in what will hopefully become a way-of-life for you and your family.

3: Water–The Essence of Life

"Water is the driving force of all nature."
-Leonardo da Vinci

In This Chapter:

- Always make water a top priority in your survival plan, second only to security and personal defense.
- Store a short-term supply of water for emergencies. Minimum two gallons per person, per day. Rotate water supplies to keep your inventory fresh.
- Have a long term water plan for an extended duration crisis.
- Suspect water must always be (treated) made safe to drink.
- Water can be disinfected by killing any organic, living, waterborne pathogens.
- The disinfection methods discussed in this book will not remove pollution or other chemical contaminates so common in urban water sources.
- Have alternate water sources, and redundant methods for making the water safe to drink.
- Recycle water for non-drinking uses. Recycled water may be used, for example, to flush toilets.

Why it Matters:

Water is the foundation for life itself. Access to safe, reliable water sources is crucial for the health and wellbeing of any society. The total amount of water in the human body is approximately 60 percent; the brain is about 70 percent water, and the lungs about 90 percent. Every cell in our body needs water to function properly. The body uses water to maintain its temperature, remove waste and to lubricate joints. Without water life is not possible. Without water your days are seriously numbered – usually three days. Although after the first day or so you will not be of much use to yourself, or anybody else. Water is an extremely serious component in any survival plan; some would say the most crucial component. Life as we know it is not possible without clean, fresh water.

There is no shortage of water on Earth; water covers about 70% of the planet's surface. Yet with all that water, less than 1% is drinkable. Ocean water is filled with salt and other minerals. Humans can't drink ocean water unless the salt is removed, and this is usually a very difficult and cost prohibitive process.

How long a person can actually survive without clean drinking water depends greatly on the circumstances. For example, a small child left in a hot car can dehydrate, overheat and die within a few hours. In a survival situation water comes in second only to security. Some people say that water is always the number one priority in any survival situation; this is partially correct. If your life is at risk from other more immediate dangers (gunfire for example) water won't be your primary consideration. But it will very quickly become your number one concern as soon as you remove yourself from the immediate threat.

Given how important water is to our survival, it's amazing just how little thought people give this precious commodity, and how easily our society wastes huge amounts of it on a daily basis. I can imagine future generations looking back at us in disbelief, and wondering what kind of people could have used perfectly good drinking water to flush their toilets, or to wash their cars?

Worldwide there are currently many countries facing serious water challenges. These problems will only get worse if they are not adequately addressed. In the near future, as the world's population continues to grow and demand begins to outstrip supply, we will probably see many wars fought between neighboring countries over water, and water rights.

Here in America we are seeing the worst drought in more than half a century affecting people in more than two thirds of the continental U.S.; cities in some of the driest states are quickly running out of water. Across the U.S., state and local government officials are initiating and enforcing emergency measures to conserve the remaining water supplies to ensure there is at least enough to drink. Some of the cities and towns most affected by the ongoing drought are in Great Plain states, but at this point it is clear that few regions will be unaffected by this ever-growing problem. Despite these very serious concerns, across the U.S., for many others it is *business as usual*; few people recognize the risks or how they would be affected, and even fewer care.

Maybe our indifferent attitude towards water reflects its perceived abundance, availability and relative low cost. For most of us, water flows freely from many sources within and outside of our homes. To many people in developing countries, where it's not unusual for folks to sometimes walk for miles carrying containers of water from the nearest well, our attitude towards water and our lack of conservation must seem absurd. Water weighs 8.35 pounds per gallon, for those of you who were wondering.

Dehydration – How do You Know?

When most of us say we are thirsty, what we really mean is that we would like a nice cool drink; preferably with lots of ice and carbonation. In general, very few of us really know what it feels like to be without water for more than a few hours. Some of us have been in the sun either working or playing, and have experienced some mild level of heatstroke and/or dehydration – it's a condition that if left untreated can very quickly become life threatening. But, rarely do most of us go for more than a few hours without having a drink of water or some other beverage. Dehydration is only the beginning of what can be a very painful death.

Some of the symptoms of dehydration may include:
- Extreme thirst
- Headache
- Confusion
- Little or no urine, or dark urine
- Dizziness

- Dry mouth
- No tears when crying

You should not wait to start seeing any of these symptoms to begin drinking water. Under normal circumstances you should be drinking 6 to 8 glasses of water per day. During survival situations you may actually need more than this due to increased stress and physical exertion. During a WCS, water may be in very short supply. At a minimum you will need at least two gallons of water per person per day - this is just for drinking. For bathing, washing, cooking, and other necessities you'll need much more.

Water in America

Cities throughout America have undergone tremendous changes in the last fifty years. As our cities have increased in size and population, so has the demand for fresh drinking water. Today, the majority of America's population (in excess of 80%), get their water from municipal water systems. In 1955 about 30 percent of American households found their own water supply by digging a well in their backyard. Today that number is closer to 12 percent and shrinking. In 1955 there were roughly 166 million people in the U.S., today there are in excess of 300 million and growing.

In most urban areas, water is usually brought in from sources many miles away. As our population continues to grow, self-reliance continues to shrink and reliance on an overextended and outdated water infrastructure continues to increase at a staggering rate. Despite an overall failing, outdated and crumbling system of water pipes, levees, water storage facilities and canals, most cities continue to expand, and an ever growing population continues to add pressure to severely strained systems. Incredibly some cities are still using the same water systems that were in use in the 1950s. Does any of this sound the least bit worrisome to you? It worries the American Society of Civil engineers, who have concluded that

"Although America spends billions on infrastructure each year, drinking water systems face an annual shortfall of at least $11 billion in funding to replace aging facilities..."

The water crisis in America is not a topic that we will tackle in this book, but if you are willing to bet your life on something, you should at least know what you're betting on. This failing, outdated and overwhelmed system is the same one you and I rely on to bring us the water we need to survive; remember three days, maybe even less.

Ask the average person what they would do if their tap water stopped flowing, and you would most likely get a blank stare, followed by a nervous laugh, an excuse and a hasty departure. That person would probably think that you were crazy. People don't expect that their tap water will ever stop flowing; and what's wrong with you for even asking such a ridiculous question? People don't imagine that the water supply may one day be contaminated or somehow be compromised. They don't even see it as a possibility to plan for.

Now ask yourself. What would you do if, for whatever reason, the water just stopped flowing even for a few days? Would you have an emergency supply of water to keep you and your family alive in the short term? Would you have an adequate plan for the long term? Would you have redundant methods for filtering and/or disinfecting suspect water? Would you have access to an alternate source of water once your emergency supplies ran out? Or would you be among the masses standing in long lines hoping that someone, anyone, would arrive with some drinking water?

In order to survive a WCS in an urban environment, your water plan will require your full attention and some substantial planning, far in advance of any unexpected event. If you're like most people, you may have a few gallons of water in your house. By now, you must realize that a few gallons of stored water will do you little good, and that your water preparations need to be a whole lot more comprehensive. You must also be thinking that you really need to get started. I couldn't agree more.

What You Should Know:

Here are some basic tips and ideas to help you get started.

- Establish and maintain a short-term supply of water for emergencies – minimum of three weeks, preferably more. Figure no less than 2 gallon per person per day, extra for needs other than drinking. Yes, I said 2 gallons, (the standard recommendation is 1 gallon, which in most situations is not enough). You will need even more if you live in a hot and humid environment. This is your first line of defense, don't neglect it. You can always look for alternate sources and either filter or disinfect the water, but your most reliable source of water will always be your short-term supply.

- Keep your water supplies current. Rotate your stock and update your inventory often. If necessary, use additives to keep your water fresh and safe. Smaller containers will make it easier to rotate, use and manage your water supplies.

- Store your water in more than one location throughout your house. You never know what can happen, or where you will be when disaster strikes. If the entire short-term water supply is in one location it is more at risk from damage or contamination in a crisis.

- Maintain a supply of empty, BPA free, drinking-safe plastic containers for storing water. These 5 to 7 gallon containers are usually stackable, easy to fill and come with a spout. Having 5 to 10 of these containers can provide you with a quick and easy way of storing treated water. Even if you keep these filled and treated for long term storage, these containers are a good investment; in addition they are compact and easy to transport.

- Fifty-five (55) gallon drum-style containers have a purpose, but for most situations they are too heavy and usually very difficult to move; smaller containers are more manageable.

- Don't forget to have a drinking water safe hose to fill your containers and a manual pump for moving water between containers.

- In addition to your stored supplies, at the first sign of trouble you should fill as many containers, pots, pans, sinks, bathtubs, and anything else that you can get your hands on with water. If the crisis is averted you can always use the water for something – water should never be wasted.

- Most crisis situations are typically short-term in duration, and your emergency supplies should be sufficient. It is usually the first few weeks that are the most difficult since the majority of people don't store sufficient water, and their limited supplies quickly run out. Always store more water than you expect to need, since unexpected friend or relatives may find their way to your home during a crisis. It's always better to have more than you anticipate needing.

- Have alternate water sources. In any extended crisis, emergency water supplies will eventually run out. In a long-term emergency situation you will need to have a plan "B". A swimming pool or spa, a hot water heater, a lake, river, etc. Scout-out your surroundings and make a map of all the possible sources of water. The closer to your home these sources are the better. (Remember 8.35 pounds per gallon). But just in case, make sure to have a low tech and inconspicuous way of moving the heavy water from point "A" to point "B" since, as you know by now, carrying it by hand will probably not be an option. A small shopping cart, a hand truck or a wheel barrel should help you in moving your containers.

- Suspect water must always be disinfected before it is safe to drink. When in doubt, filter and treat the water before drinking it. Don't take any unnecessary chances.

- Just because water is clear does not mean it is safe to drink. Even crystal clear water may contain waterborne pathogens that can make you very ill. During a WCS is not the time to get sick, and to risk some very nasty health complications.

- Have a high capacity water filter for use at your home or retreat, but also maintain a smaller portable unit for when you're on the move.

- Pre-filtering water removes most particulate matter and saves wear and tear on your water filter. Pour water through a coffee filter, towels, or a clean cotton material, such as a shirt. Water may still have a color, but using one of these methods will at least remove large particles, bugs, dirt, etc. You must still always treat/disinfect water before drinking.

- Have redundant methods for making water safe to drink. Have at least three different methods for disinfecting water. (For example boiling, or treating with bleach, Iodine, ultra-violet radiation, etc.)

    o   Clear water can be made safe to drink by boiling it for two minutes. Set it aside and let it cool. Remember not to pour disinfected water back into a container that previously held the infected water, the container must also be disinfected before you drink water out of it.

    o   Clear water can be made safe to drink by adding 2-4 drops of chlorine beach for every U.S. quart and let-ting it sit for 30-45 minutes.

    o   Clear water can be made safe to drink by adding 5-10 drops of iodine 2% for every quart and letting it sit for 30-45 minutes.

    o   Clear water can be made safe to drink by placing it in a washed, clear plastic one-two liter container and letting it sit in direct sunlight for six hours. This is called the SODIS Method. More on this later in the chapter.

- Suspect water can be disinfected by one of the methods described above which in essence kills off any organic, living, waterborne pathogens. However, the disinfection methods discussed in this book will not remove pollutants or other chemical contaminates that are common in urban water sources. These contaminates can be just as dangerous, or more dangerous, than waterborne pathogens. Explore your options well in advance of any crisis. Look around and make sure that the water source you may be considering is not a collection point for a farm or some industrial facility that may be releasing/dumping dangerous chemicals into that water.

- In a pinch you can drink the water from your toilet tank, (not bowl) water heater, pool, hot tub, it won't taste very good, but it should be safe to drink – unless... If you're a fan of blue toilet water and have been known to add chemicals to you toilet tank to make the water blue and to keep the bowl sparkling clean, don't drink the water from the toilet tank. If in doubt, don't drink it.

- Eating dehydrated food requires an increase in water intake. If your food stores include a large supply of dehydrated or freeze dried foods you will need to store extra water.

- Eating protein requires increased water intake to digest your meal.

- The water in canned food is a good source of additional hydration. Another reason to store canned foods.

- Exertion and heavy sweating will require increased water intake to keep you hydrated. Don't wait until you start feeling thirsty to begin drinking water, by then you have probably already started to dehydrate.

- If you plan in advance, you should be able to harvest some rainwater. Don't overlook this as a possible option. Make sure that your collection system and containers are drinking water safe and free of any contaminants. Outdoor systems have been known to contain mold, dirt, bugs, dead animals, and a wide variety of other really nasty stuff. Inspect your system well in advance of any crisis, and keep it functioning and in proper repair.

- Depending on where you live and the time of year, melting ice and snow are also possible sources of water.
- Never use suspect water to wash dishes, utensils, pots or pans, to brush your teeth, or to prepare any food.

What You'll Need:

- Pre-packed gallons or smaller bottles of water. Store enough water to last at least 2-3 weeks. The more the better.
- Water safe containers. Look for containers with a stackable shape to save space and for easy storage, that are BPA free, and that have a handle and spout. *Reliance Products* makes a rigid/stackable 7 Gallon container called the *Aqua-Tainer*. It features a space-saving design, has a molded grip, a hide-away spigot and is very affordable.
- Water Safe Hose (Usually white in color) – Made with FDA approved materials that are safe for drinking water. Many garden hoses are made with toxic chemicals that can leach into the water and cause serious health threats. These can be easily found in most outdoor and camping supply stores, or on-line.
- Chlorine Bleach (Unscented).
- Assortment of different sizes of funnels.
- Manual water pump(s) have at least two.
- Tincture of Iodine 2% and Povidone - Iodine Solution 10%
- Eye droppers (Have a least half a dozen).
- Coffee filters, to pre filter water.
- Large capacity water filter(s) with extra elements/filters. Consider the *Katadyn TRK Ceradyn* gravity water filter. Practical for long-term uses. This unit has three ceramic filter elements, and holds about 2.5 gallons. Also consider

the *Big Berkey* which can filter up to 30 gallons of water per day.

- Small, portable water filter for when you are on-the-move. Consider the *Katadyn Pocket Water Microfilter.* This highly portable filter uses a silver-impregnated ceramic element to produce drinkable water.
- Plastic storage/freezer bags in various sizes. Quart and gallon sizes are usually the most useful.
- Extra large, non-lubricated condoms make pretty good improvised water storage containers.
- Water that is not safe to drink may still be valuable to you for other purposes, for example to flush toilets or to wash out 5 gallon buckets that are used to dispose of waste.

The SODIS Method

SODIS is short for solar disinfection. With SODIS all you need is sunlight and a PET bottle. The UV-A rays in sunlight will kill viruses, bacteria and parasites. With this method you actually use the sun's energy to disinfect the water. This can be useful, especially if other forms of energy you would normally use to heat the water are in short supply. It's simple, easy and requires no special equipment. Here is a quick list of steps to get started:

1. Find some clear plastic bottles of the 1-2 liter size. Remove any labels or other obstructions that may block the sunlight.
2. Make sure the bottles are made from a drinking safe plastic. The bottles should be made from polyethylene terephthalate (PET). Check the bottom of the bottle for a recycling symbol with a "1" inside. Clear glass bottles can also be used. Bottles must always be clear, transparent and colorless.
3. Wash the bottle(s) well. Make sure it was never used to hold any toxic liquids.
4. Draw some water in another container and let it sit for about 30 minutes to allow sediments to settle to the bottom of the

container. Cloudy or turbid water will reduce the effectiveness of the SODIS method.

5.   Use a funnel lined with a coffee filter or a clean cotton cloth to pour the water into the plastic bottle. Pre-filtering the water will help to remove any additional debris. Coffee filters are cheap, disposable and easy to use.

6.   Find a good location where the sun is strong. Place your bottle down horizontally to increase the surface area the sun will cover and let it sit for no less than six hours. A dark surface will absorb more of the sun's energy and produce more heat.

7.   After six hours remove the bottle from the sun and let it cool before drinking.

8.   The disinfected water should be consumed from the same container in which it was disinfected, or from a container or cup that is known to be clean and safe. Pouring disinfected water into a container that previously held suspect water will increase the chances of contaminating the water all over again.

9.   This method will not work if it is overcast of rainy. If it rains, just collect the rainwater in a clean container. Rainwater is usually safe to drink unless it has otherwise been contaminated.

Having a strong water plan is one of your top priorities in a disaster situation. Maintaining adequate stores of clean, fresh water will act as your first line of defense. Having a short-term supply, as well as alternate sources of water and redundant methods of disinfecting water will ensure your physical wellbeing, and your peace of mind.

4: Food–The Short and the Long of it

"Civilization as it is known today could not have evolved, nor can it survive, without an adequate food supply."
-Norman Borlaug

In This Chapter:
- We're all in for a big reality check.
- Our food supply chain is fragile.
- Food during and after a WCS.
- What to store, and how to store it.
- During a crisis it's all about the calories.
- Buy and store foods that you are willing to eat on a daily basis.
- Store foods that you currently eat. During a WCS is no time to introduce an entirely new menu to your digestive system.
- Store some extended shelf-life foods that are ready-to-eat with minimum preparation and that don't require additional water or any cooking.
- Plan on warming food, but avoid cooking or any other activities that will call unwanted attention to your group or its location. Keep it as simple as possible.
- Variety goes a long way, store different kinds of foods.
- Keep it fresh - rotate, rotate, rotate.
- Be mindful of food allergies and other medical considerations for members of your group.
- Have a plan, keep an accurate inventory; take the time and effort to store food properly to avoid spoilage or contamination.

Where We Are:

In the United States, as in many other developed nations, the majority of the population is used to eating far more calories than they need to maintain body weight or to stay healthy. Inexpensive pre-package, ready-to-eat, and fast food choices are the norm, and can be easily and conveniently found just about everywhere. Few of us ever stop to appreciate how simple it is to get something to eat. Grabbing a meal is fast, easy and for the most part relatively inexpensive.

Although too much of what we eat is over-processed junk, loaded with fat, sugar, salt and empty calories, a full belly keeps us from any uncomfortable feelings of hunger. To be more accurate, what many of us call hunger, is really just an expectation based on the time of day – "its noontime let's go have lunch". What we often confuse with the feeling of hunger is just anxiety or sometimes even thirst, since most of us don't drink nearly enough water. People sometimes also eat out of boredom and often just because food is so accessible, and it tastes good. Many of us can't resist the instant gratification we get from food.

Food manufactures have found many inventive ways to make very inexpensive chemicals, additives, and fillers taste really good. If most people knew what they were truly eating, they probably wouldn't eat it. Poor eating habits, junk food and the never-ending super-duper-sized portions take a major toll on our health and drastically reduce the effectiveness of our body's immune system. But, as long as "food" continues to be tasty, convenient and relatively inexpensive, few people will complain, or consider changing their eating habits.

In the U.S. it's not unusual for a typical meal to easily top 4000 calories, with a generous serving of 100-150 grams of fat. (An average person is supposed to consume maybe 2,000 calories per day, and 60 or 70 fat grams.) If, on the other hand, you are very active or have a job that requires long hours of physical exertion, you may actually need more calories. The general idea is to keep a balance between how many calories go in, and how many are used by the body. Whatever calories you don't burn up, will usually get stored as fat — over the long-term this can really add up.

During normal times being over-weight, and under-healthy can affect your quality of life. A crisis will usually subject most people to tremendous stress and hardship, both physical and mental. If your body and immune system is already challenged by excess weight and poor health, you will start out at an incredible disadvantage. And just when you need your health and stamina the most, your body may not be up to the task.

The Supply Chain and Other Threats

Most of the food that makes its way to us urban folks comes by truck. This vital transportation system is responsible for the majority of the food distribution to urban areas. But as we all know a fast, efficient trucking system depends on the road system, the availability of fuel, and an army of people and computers to process the loads so that everything reaches the marketplace in a timely manner. If this transportation system is somehow compromised, or stops functioning altogether, the entire food supply chain grinds to a halt. (Think natural and manmade disasters, social unrest, bad weather, grid failure, fuel shortages, pandemic, cyber attack, etc.) All it takes is one natural or manmade crisis to potentially throw the entire system into chaos.

During a WCS, food deliveries may be disrupted, or may stop altogether — even a short-term disruption can be disastrous. Most retailers maintain little or no in-store inventory — usually 72 hours or less of food on their shelves. Retailers re-stock their stores based on daily deliveries; this helps them save money and allows them to order only what they need. The Down side of this streamlined system is that the moment the trucks stop rolling the shelves will be empty almost immediately. Without transportation the farmers, producers and wholesalers can't get their products to the stores and the entire system can very quickly collapse with little or no warning. Under these conditions, we can expect to see plenty of panic buying/hoarding, civil disruptions and an overall increase in violence among the public, as people fight for the last scraps on the shelves.

Within a few days of any major crisis, our society can potentially go from vast food abundance, variety and availability to empty store shelves and crowds of angry people desperately struggling to find something to eat. These will be the very same people that just a few days before ate their fill, with few limitations and never gave food, or its availability, a second thought. Imagine how most of them will deal with this new and very harsh reality. Although these shortages may only be temporary, when people are hungry and they realize that the store shelves are empty and restaurants are all closed, a few days will seem like an eternity. Those who didn't make at least some minimum preparations may find themselves in a world of pain.

Given our nation's obsession with food, the mindless indulgence, and our self-professed freedom to be irresponsible, shortages of food will be a tremendous physical and psychological adjustment; an adjustment that most people will not be able to make easily. History has shown us, time and again, that hungry people are desperate people, and desperate people do desperate things. Our society is not used to doing without - people expect to eat on a daily basis. Imagine how these folks will react when food becomes scarce – even in the short-term.

There is not much, if anything, that we can do about how other people live their lives. But, our first and only priority must be the health and welfare of our own family. If nothing else, we must make sure that we are able to feed ourselves and our loved ones in the event of a crisis.

Survival is a Calories Game

Calories are the basic units of energy contained in all foods. Our bodies need this energy to maintain the body's vital functions. How many calories a person needs to maintain body weight and to function depends on many factors, including age, gender, and the amount of lean muscle mass. Not eating sufficient calories for an extended period of time causes weight loss, muscle loss, and eventually organ failure and death. During *normal* times, responsible people try to eat reasonable portions of wholesome foods that will help them maintain a strong healthy body, and to avoid becoming overweight. During a crisis when food supplies are compromised, you won't find too many people worried about overeating; primarily because food will not be abundant. Those who have no food reserves will be in a panic. Those who have stored food will begin to carefully ration their supplies in anticipation of a prolonged disruption. Even during a short-term crisis, most folks will find themselves stressed and physically exerting their bodies in ways that they are not used to. During a WCS you'll need a mix of carbohydrates, protein, fats vitamins, minerals and electrolytes to stay on your game. The moment you start to reduce your caloric intake, you will also begin to see a marked decline in your physical and mental performance. It's your job to make sure you plan ahead so that this doesn't happen to you.

Where to Start

Formulating a food plan and putting it into action can seem over-whelming, especially if you've never done it before. There are many options, and many things to consider, but you shouldn't make it any more complicated than it has to be. One way to get started is to take it step-by-step and to build on your efforts as you learn more, and get more comfortable with the process. Your first goal should be to have a manageable supply of food, that stores well and that can be used and rotated on a regular basis.

Very few people have the time, money, space or even the desire to purchase, store and manage many years worth of food. And rightly so, preparations on that level can be a monumental task, requiring lots of time and money that many people just don't have. In addition, that much food would also necessitate a very large storage area, proper storage conditions, rotation and ongoing management. For urban residents, who are already living in limited space, storing that much food may be next to impossible.

Baring some sort of apocalyptic event, most urban survival and/ or crisis situations will usually be relatively short-term in nature. Realistically, most of us will not be planning for events that will last for years, or even months. Few of us can reasonably store that much food, water or other supplies. Short-term usually refers to any period of time between a few days to a month. Longer than that, and people in urban areas will begin to face some really big challenges; challenges that won't be overcome just be storing additional food. The idea is to have enough food to allow you and your family to survive a short-term crisis within the relative safety of your own home or some other secure location. This goal can be realistically accomplished with some advance planning, and without having to rent a warehouse or take out a second mortgage.

I am not suggesting that you short-change your food storage program. Everyone should store as much food as they are able to afford, and manage properly. If you have enough space, enough money and the necessary amount of time, you will be able to accomplish far more than someone who is limited by time, money or space. The key message here is that no matter how limited your space or budget, there will always be room for improvement. What's important is that you make the most effective and efficient use of what you have available to you.

Buy What You Regularly Eat, and Rotate Your Stores

It is important to store food items that you regularly eat; and to rotate your supplies on an ongoing basis. There are many reasons for doing this, here are a few.

- Allows you to always have the freshest food possible. If you buy, store and forget, your food will expire, get stale or will lose substantial nutritional value well before you ever get to eat it. In some situations you will end up throwing most of it out. It's a waste of money, but worse yet; imagine that a crisis happens and the food supplies you were relying on have spoiled.

- Allows you to make sure the food you store agrees with your digestive system, and will not create any dietary issues when you suddenly start eating a much different menu during a crisis. Storing foods that you are not familiar with is a recipe for disaster.

- Buying food that you only plan on eating in an emergency will ensure that you will have many unpleasant surprises at the worst possible time. Besides digestive issues, you may have food allergies that you may not even know about. During a WCS is the worse time to have a possible life threatening allergic reaction.

- Familiarity with the foods you store will ensure that you know how to properly cook these foods when the time comes. (Remember your food stores should include mostly items that don't require cooking). For those situations when cooking may be okay, keep it very simple and make sure that you have the right ingredients and know how to use them. During a crisis, going to the supermarket will not be an option.

- Eating foods that you are familiar with will bring you and your family a certain sense of comfort during times of high stress.

- Easy on the family budget. There is no need to go out and buy large quantities of any one food product. It's better to just buy extra items each time you go shopping and build up your supplies. The new items simply get rotated, and you use the oldest products first.

- Helps spread out the risk of spoilage. For example, if you make a large purchase of tomato sauce, all at onetime, your entire purchase will probably have the same expiration date. If you had staggered your purchases over time, at any given point, you will have an inventory with expiration dates spread out over a period of time. In other words, your entire inventory doesn't expire at the same time.

- Lastly, sometimes products are contaminated or otherwise tainted when they leave the processing facility or factory. These products get into the marketplace often necessitating a product recall; but almost never before many people use the tainted products and get sick. If you are unlucky and happen to buy the contaminated product in large quantities, you may be stuck with an unusable product at the worst possible time.

What Foods to Store and Why

During a crisis, you and your family may eat foods that you are familiar with, but you will eat them in a much different way. You will be stressed physically and mentally, and your body will need additional calories for energy. Fresh meats, fruits, vegetables and dairy products will most likely not be available to you. And even if fresh produce was available, you could not eat enough fruits and vegetables to give you the energy you need in a survival scenario – you'll need calorie dense foods.

During a crisis, you will almost certainly be limited to foods that are canned, or pre-packaged. This does not mean that you should store junk, on the contrary; you should try to store foods that are high in quality calories and nutrition. Your main goal should be to provide your body with calorie rich foods that will sustain you. Calorie dense foods are those that contain a fairly large amount of calories for their relative portion size. Since many of the foods that you would normally eat may not be available, you will need to store foods that will nonetheless provide the calories and nutrition your body needs to keep going without having to eat unreasonably large quantities of food.

A word of caution: before you go out and buy any food products in quantity, make sure to test them to ensure that you actually like what you are buying, and that your digestive system agrees. If it doesn't taste good you will not eat it. If your body does not digest these foods well, you will be miserable. And finally, if you are allergic to any of these products, you will not be able to eat them. In any event, you may find yourself throwing-out hundreds, maybe even thousands of dollars worth of food. Taste and test before you commit to more than a small amount.

Also, try to stay away from the mega size containers of any one product. Mega sizes appear to be a great deal since the portion sizes are less expensive then when you buy a smaller container. But, and this is a very big "but" it only makes sense to buy those big portions if you actually use the entire contents of the package. If you buy a huge container of some product only to throw most of it out because it was way too much for you to use before it spoiled, then it won't seem like such a good deal anymore.

The Food List

Here are some examples of calorie-rich foods that store relatively well without refrigeration. You should consider these foods, and other similar foods with high caloric/nutritional values, for your core food storage supplies.

- Peanut Butter – 100 grams of peanut butter provides almost 600 calories, over 21 grams of protein and a respectable amount of vitamins and minerals. Peanut butter stores well and requires no heat and/or any preparation. It taste good and can be eaten many different ways, including right out of the jar. Load up on this.

- Almond Butter – Less common than peanut butter. Almond butter is more expensive and sometimes does not store as long. This may be a viable alternative if you don't like, or are allergic to peanut butter. Still a very good option that is packed with nutrition and good solid calories.

- Pasta – Provides lots of carbohydrates and although you need water to prepare it, pasta can be made in many different ways and once cooked can be eaten hot or cold.

- Pasta sauces – In the event that you are able to cook pasta you will need to put something on it. Precooked pasta sauces can make plain pasta into a complete meal. There are literally dozens of different sauces to choose from and most will store well for long periods of time.

- Canned macaroni & cheese, ravioli, spaghetti, tortellini, shells, with beef, cheese or a variety of other flavors. The idea is to be able to open a can, heat it up or not, and eat it without any fuss or cooking. These meals are relatively inexpensive, and most children love them. Watch for high sodium content since too much sodium will increase thirst, and water intake requirements.

- Tuna – Canned in water, one can (165g) of tuna has about 200 calories and over 42g of protein. Tuna can be eaten right out of the can, and added to other ingredients to enhance the meal. Look for the foil pouches if you want a more portable container.

- Sardines – Canned in oil sardines; have about 200 calories and about 23g of protein. A good source of calcium and protein. Also look for sardines canned in tomato sauce.

- Chicken – (140g) of chicken provides about 24g of protein and 140 calories. Also provides some variety in your menu.

- Salmon – Canned (140g) of salmon provides about 85g of protein and 200 calories. Also provides some variety in your menu.

- Canned Meats – There are many varieties available including pork, beef, hams, turkey, etc. Sample some of the different types and brands and buy a variety of the ones you like best. Watch the sodium content on these.

- Other Canned Seafood – Oysters, clams, mussels. Not everyone's first choice, but still good solid options.

- Soups, Stews, Hash & Chili – If you have the time and don't mind the effort consider making and canning your own. Otherwise, buy a variety of off-the-shelf products.

- Sweet peas, whole kernel corn, sweet corn, creamed corn, spinach, French style beans, mushrooms – never as good as the fresh stuff, but in a survival situation they will add much needed variety and some additional nutrition to your meals.

- Rice – White rice stores better and keeps longer than other types of rice. 158g of cooked white rice has about 200 calories and 4g of protein. Also store a supply of instant rice for situations where cooking is not an option - just add some hot water and eat.

- Beans – Canned beans can be warmed up and eaten right out of the can, or jazzed up with pork, beef or sausage. Choose black, white, lentils, Lima, pinto, navy, kidney, black-eyed, chickpeas. Also consider baked beans - which come in many flavors. Rice and beans makes for the complete protein dish providing all the essential amino acids needed to survive. Cooking raw beans from scratch is not recommended in a survival scenario since uncooked beans require long cooking times and usually involve much more time, effort and cooking energy.

- Oats – Oats are a concentrated source of fiber and nutrients. Can be eaten alone or used to add extra nutrition to other meals. Instant is easiest to prepare, regular has better consistency.

- Honey – An age-old food that dates back thousands of years and has an indefinite shelf-life. Use it as a sweetener, or an energy booster. One ounce of honey has about 127 calories.

- Evaporated and Sweetened Condensed Milk – Shelf-stable canned milk products made by removing about half of the water from milk; the evaporation process also concentrates the nutrients and food energy. When mixed with equal parts water become the rough equivalent of fresh milk. Sweetened condensed has added sugar. Widely used during the early 1900s when refrigeration was not yet common. Taste pretty good and stores very well.

- Instant Powdered Milk – Excellent source of calcium, protein and vitamins. Stores well and reconstitutes with water.

Can store for 3-5 years in cans. Use it to drink, or to add extra nutrition to other foods. Taste is sometimes an issue with some brands; add a few drops of vanilla extract or chocolate powder to improve.

- Dark Chocolate – 70-85% cacao solids, a (101g) bar has about 8g of protein and 600 calories. A good nutritious treat that keeps well and tastes great.
- Raisins, prunes and other dried fruits – Store well, taste good, loaded with nutrition, and require no preparation. Can also be used to add flavor and additional nourishment to other foods or eaten as a nutritious snack.
- Granola Bars – One bar usually provides 100+ calories, 5g protein, and 24g carbohydrates. By themselves these are usually insufficient as a meal, but make great snacks, store well and come in a variety of flavors. Also good for bug-out-bag.
- Protein Bars – Some protein bars have in excess of 500 calories, 45g of protein, and 50g of carbohydrates. I would not make it a habit of eating these on a daily basis, but during a WCS they have everything you need to keep your energy levels high. They are lightweight, handy, and packed full of good nutrition. Store some of these for meal replacement, and have some handy for you bug-out-bag.
- Nuts and Seeds – Almonds, cashews, walnuts, peanuts and sunflower seeds contain about 200 calories per ounce. They are calorie-dense but also packed with muscle building protein, healthy fats, fiber and vitamins, including potassium, vitamin E, zinc, and magnesium. Good snack and morale booster.
- Processed fruit in cans or jars – Again, never as good as the fresh stuff, but pretty good nonetheless. Store peaches, pears, pineapple, fruit cocktail, mandarin slices, and a variety of other options. Products packed in natural juices can also help with hydration since you can drink the juice.

- Fruit Juices in cans or boxes – Handy and delicious, an easy way to drink some additional tasty calories.

- Pancake mix and syrup – When cooking is an option, pancakes and maple syrup can be great comfort food; packed with tons of calories (2 pancakes with syrup have over 500 calories). Yet another inexpensive calorie dense food that stores well and tastes great.

- Olive Oil – Good for cooking, dressings, or for adding flavor to foods. One table spoon contains about 120 calories. Keeps well. Easy way to add flavor and nutrition to pasta, meats, beans, canned vegetables, and other foods.

- Protein Powder/Meal Replacement Drinks – One scoop (44g) of premium protein powder mixed with water will provide 200 calories, over 20g of quality protein, fiber, potassium and carbohydrates. To increase your protein intake mix with milk. (See powdered, condensed or evaporated milk above). Protein powders usually store well, taste very good and come in a variety of flavors. This is the same stuff used by body builders and elite athletes to supplement their protein intake. A quick and easy way to supplement your meals or use it as a meal replacement. Either way it will provide you with some very high quality nutrition; really good stuff to have around. Keep some in your bug-out-bag.

- Instant coffee – Even in the middle of a crisis people will want their coffee, and if it makes them feel better, why not? There are some very upscale (another word for expensive) instant coffees that have hit the market in the last few years. Freeze dried national brands will probably do just as well at a much lower cost. Nothing beats fresh brewed, but in a pinch good old instant coffee will hit the spot and deliver some much needed caffeine. A cup of coffee will also help lift the morale in any group. For those gourmet types that insist on freshly brewed coffee – take note: The smell of coffee brewing carries for very long distances. Stick to instant and keep it low-key. Coffee is certainly not calorie dense, but it's important nonetheless.

This list is intended to help you get started. Are there many more foods we could have added to this list? Absolutely! Entire books can be written just on the topic of survival food, and the food lists would be endless. Remember this is your food supply, and you should buy and store whatever kinds of food you and your family like to eat. Just keep in mind that whatever foods you decide on, they should always be 1) shelf-stable, and store well over extended periods of time, 2) easy to prepare and consume without making a big deal, 3) generally require no cooking, can be eaten cold, or warmed up slightly, 4) fit nicely within you budget, and 5) easy to rotate and use on a regular basis.

Note: If you plan on storing canned foods, you will need to have at least two (2) very reliable, manual can openers. I have tested many can openers over the years – most have failed to stand up to everyday use.   The best, most reliable can opener I have ever used is the *zyliss* "lock-n-lift" can opener. The *zyliss* bites down on the can and won't let go until the can is open. The powerful cutting wheel opens cans of all sizes with minimum effort. It also features a magnet lid lifter that lifts up the lid to avoid accidents. Having a good can opener during a WCS is not optional, it's a necessity. The *zyliss* "lock-n-lift" costs about $15.00 retail, but it's worth every penny.

Just-Add Water Meals

Some people love the prepackaged, camping-style pouch foods. They provide a quick and easy meal for emergencies or to carry over long distances. They are lightweight and can be prepared in minutes. Just add some hot water, let it sit for a few minutes and eat your hot meal right out of the pouch. These meals can be expensive and some would say that they are an acquired taste. Many people love the convenience, but not always the cost. Some meals taste much better than others; experiment with a few pouches or get an assortment and check them out.

It used to be that you had to order these meals on-line or go to a camping or sporting goods store to find them, today even the big box retailers and club stores carry them. Expect to pay from $5.00 to $10.00 per pouch, depending on size and type of meal. Because they are lightweight and can be eaten right out of the pouch, I would consider these for a bug-out bag, but not for the core sheltering-in-place supplies – they're simply too expensive.

Meals, Ready-to-Eat

The Meal, Ready-to-Eat (MREs) is a self-contained field ration that has traditionally been used by the military in combat, not only because it packs lots of nutrition and calories but, because these meals are precooked and can be eaten right out of the pouch. They can be eaten cold, but taste much better warm. (Some MREs come with a built-in heater pack). MREs have an estimated shelf life of approximately 5 years if kept at an ideal temperature of 50 °F, the higher the temperature the shorter the shelf life.

An MRE is a complete meal usually consisting of an entree, a side, a dessert, a drink mix, instant coffee/tea, bread or a biscuit, jelly, peanut butter, cheese, hard candy, and an accessory pack containing plastic utensils, salt, pepper a napkin, wet wipe, matches, toilet paper, and a food warmer. There are a number of different brands of MREs and prices range from very reasonable to the ridiculous. Shop around and whenever possible try to buy them locally since this will save you the shipping fees that sometimes can be rather expensive.

MREs should have a place in your survival plan as a bug-out food or to keep in your get-home-bag or the survival auto pack. As with the pouch-style meals I would not consider them for my core bugging-in stores; they are simply too expensive. If you decide to stock up on these, remember, even MREs need to be rotated. They have an extended, but not an unlimited shelf life. So be prepared to eat some MREs, or to eventually throw them out.

Long-Term Food Storage Kits

If money is no object, and you don't want to take the time to do much planning you may be tempted to go out and simply buy a prepackaged supply of food from one of many national vendors. Depending on the manufacturer, contents and quantity of actual food, these packages can cost many thousands of dollars. Most people who buy these packages have no idea what they actually contain, how the foods will taste, or how to prepare the individual components. There are suppliers that will sell you a one year supply of food consisting of 2000 calories per day for one person. This is over 200 #10 cans (a #10 can is approximately 6" wide by 7" high, and holds approximately 12 cups) of food, in almost 40 cardboard cases, for just under $4,000.00 – this is just for one person. For a family of three the total tab would be well over $12,000.00. I know few people that have the room to store 120 cases of food, and fewer still that can afford to spend upwards of $12,000.00 in one shot. Much of the food contained in these kits is uncooked and still needs to be prepared in order to be eaten. Not only do you have to store, organize and become familiar with the contents of your kit, but you must also learn to prepare all of these unfamiliar ingredients. If you are unable to cook or lack the skills necessary to process the kit's raw ingredients into an actual meal, then having these supplies becomes more of a burden, than a benefit. If you decide to go this route, make sure that you are entirely comfortable with:

- Spending many thousands of dollars, all at once.
- Buying products you may not be familiar with.
- Storing hundreds of boxes and organizing/rotating their contents.
- The quality and the taste of the products.
- Processing, cooking and preparation of the products.
- Having the ability, time and inclination to process and cook large amounts of food during a crisis.

- Cooking during a crisis without fear that your activities will draw unwanted and dangerous attention to you and your location.
- Rotating and using components from your stored kit on an ongoing basis to incorporate into your daily menu.

Remember, no matter how well it is packed or preserved, food will eventually expire, go stale, get old and/or lose its nutritional value. If you don't rotate, there will eventually come a time when your supplies will need to be discarded and replaced with fresh supplies. At that point you will be throwing out thousands of dollars worth of food, and then you need to replace it.

If you decide to buy one of these kits make sure to do your research and also request various samples of the products contained in the kit. Try the samples and make sure you like the food before you order the full package. Also shop around and compare prices, don't forget to factor in the shipping costs. Also make sure that you have a large storage area in your house that is not susceptible to moisture, insects, rodents, or wide variations in temperature or moisture/humidity.

Food Storage Mistakes

Here are some of the most common mistakes people make when planning their food storage program. (No particular order).

- Failing to have an actual food plan.
- Failing to buy foods that store well without refrigeration.
- Storing foods in locations susceptible to moisture, insects, rodents, or wide variations in temperature.
- Buying and storing food that they don't normally eat.
- Buying, storing and forgetting.
- Buying and storing foods without first trying and experimenting with these new items when cooking regular meals.
- Failing to rotate food stores.

- Failing to clearly label all boxes and/or containers to allow identification of contents and to track packaging and expiration dates.
- Storing foods that require too much preparation and complicated cooking.
- Not having the proper equipment to process food stores. For example storing whole wheat and not having a hand grinder.
- Failing to have functioning non-electric kitchen devices, such as a manual can opener, a manual mixer, etc.
- Failing to incorporate variety into their storage program.
- Failing to sample foods before buying large quantities.
- Failing to store adequate supplies of flavorings, spices, oils and common condiments necessary to prepare even the most basic meal.
- Failing to set-up an appropriate, designated area with adequate shelves or storage units to keep supplies off of the floor.
- Failing to store their supplies in durable, food-safe storage containers that will keep the food fresh, safe and away from critters, mold, mildew and other potential contaminants.
- Failing to take appropriate precautions when self-packaging food stores in long-term containers. For example using food grade liners and oxygen absorbers before putting food in plastic containers.
- Failing to keep an appropriate balance when making food purchase.
- Buying extra large quantities of basic food items because they found a good deal, even though they will never be able to consume such quantities before they spoil.
- Buying a lot of one particular item, to the exclusion of others.

- Buying large, long-term packages/kits without knowing what the kits contain or without assessing the quality of the kit's components.
- Failing to maintain a reliable inventory listing of all supplies, and updating the list periodically. Knowing what you have, and don't have, is crucial to avoid waste, duplication or worst of all having to do without something important you thought you had, but didn't.
- Trying to do it all at once. Food storage is an ongoing effort and commitment, there is no *do it all and forget it* option that works.
- Doing some great planning, but failing to ever take the first step to turn the plan into action.

5: First Aid and Medical Preparedness–
The First Line of Defense

In This Chapter:

- Every home needs a well-stocked first aid kit, and basic emergency medical supplies.
- Have a home first aid kit for everyday use.
- Have a basic kit and an expanded kit that remains untouched expect for true emergency situations.
- Have a first aid kit in your car that's specifically adapted to where you live, work and travel.
- Have a tactical trauma kit for extreme emergencies and life threatening bleeds.
- Make the kits yourself. Know what supplies are in them and how to use those supplies.
- Store at least 90 days of commonly used medications and prescription drugs that you and your family take.
- Track expirations dates and rotate stores on all medications and supplies.
- Have everyone in your group take a class in CPR and basic first aid.
- Have at <u>least</u> one person in your group trained to deal with pre-hospital trauma life support and violent force injuries.
- Maintain a strong & healthy body to avoid medical issues during a crisis.
- Maintain dental health for strong teeth, to avoid infections, gum disease and other medical complications.
- Stay current on all recommended vaccinations.
- Take a high quality multivitamin to provide your body with necessary vitamins and minerals. Also maintain a current stock of vitamins for use during an extended WCS.

Accidents and injuries are a reality of life. Like it or not, the unexpected will happen and usually the only thing you can do is to be prepared. A first aid kit is designed to treat either a non-emergency situation that does not require a doctor or hospital, but may still require care to avoid complications, or to treat an emergency situation that require instant care until the person can be taken to a doctor or hospital. In either situation, it's important to have a well-stocked first aid kit readily available and set-up for immediate use. A prudent individual will usually have various kits, each strategically situated and designed for their intended purpose. For example, a person may have a home kit, one for their car, another for the workplace and sometimes even a very small highly portable kit that they always carry on their person.

In the aftermath of a WCS, medical assistance including hospital emergency rooms, may be inaccessible for hours, days maybe even weeks. During any such disaster, having a viable first aid kit, and knowing how to use it, may help you save a life – maybe even your own.

It's true that most people have a first aid kit sitting around somewhere; *somewhere* could be at the bottom of a heap of dirty clothes on a closet floor, or maybe under a sink in a humid bathroom. The kit may be brand new, or it may be old, outdated, expired and largely empty; its contents long ago raided by family members. Regardless of its condition, if you can't find your kit quickly, or if you don't know how to use its contents effectively, your kit is probably useless anyway.

For a first aid kit to be of any benefit it must meet the following criteria:

1. You must know where it is, and it should always be kept in the same location – if it's been moved, knowing where it was last week won't help you today, especially in a true emergency.

2. The kit must be current, well stocked and filled with sufficient quantities of relevant supplies.

3. You, or someone in your group, must know how to use the supplies your kit contains.

4.   Your kit must be relevant to the potential situations you will encounter, and your level of medical training.

Commercial First Aid Kits

The biggest problem with buying a pre-made kit is that once you get it home you will most likely put it away and forget about it. The day you need it, you will have to start exploring the contents and hopefully it will contain what you need. While it's true that there are some very high quality kits on the market, they are usually expensive. There are also some kits that are filled with a lot of fancy packaging and very few truly useful products. Commercial kits may be a good place to start, but you will need to become familiar with the contents and add items that are relevant to your particular needs. Where you live and work will dictate what your kit should contain, since someone who lives and works in an urban area will have very different needs than someone who spends most of their time in a more rural environment. It's better to buy a commercial kit than to have nothing at all; but, your goal should be to make your own kit.

Make Your Own Kit

You can search far and wide for that perfect kit and you probably will never find it for one very good reason; it doesn't exist. Your needs are different than my needs. A kit that works for you, may not necessarily work for me. The idea of having a kit at all is to make sure that you have the supplies you need, and that you have them at a moment's notice. This is a process that takes time, money, planning and thought. Getting a bag and throwing in a bunch of generic supplies is probably better than having nothing at all, since there will probably be something in the bag that comes in handy – but having a few things come in handy should not be your goal. Your aim should be to compile a bag that contains items that are suited to your exact needs - Items that you have hand-selected and tested.

Your best bet is to make your own kit. You can certainly buy a basic kit and build on it; that's up to you. But the time you spend buying supplies and putting the kit together yourself will be time well spent. The more familiar you are with your kit and the use of its contents, the more valuable your kit becomes to you and your group.

The following is a list of the recommended items for a basic and an expanded kit. But don't stop there, this should be only the beginning; building and maintaining a functioning kit is an ongoing process of experimentation and evolution. Get yourself a good quality first responder's bag with lots of room and many different compartments and just get started. Here's some of what you may want in your kit:

- **Basic First Aid Kit**
  a. C-A-T Combat Application Tourniquet – True one-handed tourniquet proven to be 100% effective, by U.S. Army's Institute of Surgical Research, in completely stopping blood flow of an extremity in the event of a traumatic wound with significant hemorrhage.
  b. Celox First Aid Traumatic Wound Treatment – High performance hemostatic granules that you pour directly on a wound to stop lethal bleeding fast.
  c. Celox V12090 – Blood Clotting Granule applicator and plunger set. Helps stop bleeding from a small penetrating wound. (Knife or gunshot wounds)
  d. Gauze Pads – (4X4-inch) Larges pads to clean, compress, and dress wounds quickly and effectively.
  e. Triangular Bandage - Multi-purpose bandage to compress various injuries, support sprains or broken bones. Can also be used as an arm sling.
  f. Tactical Trauma Dressing, Israeli Bandage – Applies direct pressure for stopping bleeding in a hemorrhage wound.
  g. Steri-Strip Wound Closure Strips – A sterile wound closing system.

h. Tegaderm Transparent Film – Dressing designed for protecting skin and wound sites.

i. Nitrile Exam Gloves - Disposable latex-free gloves.

j. Adhesive Bandages - Selection of all different sizes.

k. First Aid Tape – Plain waterproof first aid tape in various sizes.

l. Elastic Bandage 3" – Supports injured body parts and provides compression where needed.

m. Triple Antibiotic Ointment – Treats and prevents infections in minor cuts, scrapes, or burns on your skin.

n. Burn Jel – Soothes cools and temporarily relieves pain due to minor burns.

o. Povidone-Iodine 10% – Gold standard of external disinfectants, kills germs in minor burns, cuts and scrapes.

p. Alcohol Prep Pads – Used to clean and sanitize, easy to store and use.

q. CPR Face Shield – Lets you give mouth-to-mouth without the risk of contamination.

r. Ibuprofen – For Pain and inflammation.

s. Acetaminophen – Lowers fevers and relieves pain.

t. Aspirin – For after a suspected heart attack.

u. Instant Cold Compress – Back-up plan for pain and inflammation if no ice is available.

v. OxyContin – This is for really serious pain – highly addictive and dangerous if misused. *(You should consult with your doctor before taking any prescription medication, and you'll need a prescription).**

w. Ciprofloxacin – A broad-spectrum antibiotic to attack bacteria. The big gun for bacterial infections. *(You should consult with your doctor before taking any prescription medication, and you'll need a prescription).**

x.   Imodium – Stops diarrhea that can cause life-threat-
     ening dehydration.

y.   Tempa-Dot Disposable Thermometers - Sterile single
     use clinical thermometers are lightweight, accurate
     and disposable. Used by NASA in space shuttles.

z.   Nuun Portable Electrolyte Hydration – Simple solu-
     tion to address a very serious issue. Active Hydration
     tablets dissolve in water and are easy to use. Comes in
     lots of different flavors.

aa. First Aid Accessories -– At least one small flashlight
     with extra batteries. Hands-free headlamp works great
     for many situations. Shears, bandage scissors, forceps.

- **Expanded First Aid Kit (Beyond the Basics)**
  Medical Supplies:

  a.   IV Fluids and needles (Different Sizes)

  b.   Sutures (Different Sizes) – Have a variety. Even if you
       don't know how to suture, you may need these for
       someone in your group who does. Or better yet, start
       learning how to do it yourself.

  c.   Needle Holders, Suture Scissors and Forceps – Good
       to have.

  d.   Antibiotics – For various situations. *(You should con-
       sult with your doctor before taking any prescription
       medication, and you'll need a prescription).**

       1.   Ciprofloxacin: used to treat or prevent anthrax
            among other things, again this is the heavy duty
            stuff.

       2.   Amoxicillin: a penicillin antibiotic used to treat
            many different types of infections caused by bac-
            teria.

       3.   Erythromycin: used to treat bronchitis, diphthe-
            ria, legionnaires disease, pertussis, pneumonia,

rheumatic fever, venereal disease, ear, intestine, lung urinary tract, and skin infections. Is sometimes used in penicillin-allergic patients instead of Amoxicillin.

4.   Co-trimoxazole: Eliminates bacteria that cause infections of the urinary tract, lungs, ears and intestines, (travelers' diarrhea).

5.   Doxycycline: Fights bacteria in the body. Often used to treat pneumonia, Lyme disease, skin infections, anthrax, urinary tract infections, and to prevent malaria.

e.   Epinephrine injection – used to treat life-threatening allergic reactions caused by insect bites, foods, medications, latex and other causes.   (You'll need a prescription, and you'll also need to know how to use it properly)*.

f.   Blood Pressure Set – Quality cuff and stethoscope. If you don't know how to take a person's blood pressure the old fashioned way, now is a good time to learn.

g.   Resuscitation Bag – Used to provide ventilation when a person's breathing is insufficient or has ceased completely.

h.   Eye Pads – Used to bandage eye injuries.

i.   Eye Wash – Sterile irrigating solution for emergency eye cleansing.

j.   Activated Charcoal – To treat poisonings, and reduce intestinal gas.

k.   Moleskin – To cover and protect blisters and sensitive skin.

l.   Berman Oral Airway Kit – Single use, latex-free

m.   Stay Alert Gum – To help you stay awake.

n.   Aluminum Splint – Help support and immobilize limbs.

The following is a list of the recommended items for a Tactical Trauma kit. This is a limited purpose kit. The primary reason to have this kit is to address serious trauma such as gunshot and knife wounds, or other life threatening bleeds. Get yourself a small zippered bag that can be attached to a belt or carried separately. The contents are limited but all are important. Here's what you'll want in your kit:

- **Tactical Trauma Kit**
    a.   C-A-T Combat Application Tourniquet.
    b.   Celox First Aid Traumatic Wound Treatment.
    c.   Celox V12090 – Blood Clotting Granule applicator and plunger set.
    d.   Gauze Pads – (4X4-inch)
    e.   Triangular Multi-purpose Bandage.
    f.   Nitrile Exam Gloves - Disposable latex-free gloves.
    g.   Elastic Bandage 3"
    h.   Israeli Battle Bandage 4"
    i.   Chest Seal – For the management of penetrating chest wounds.

*NOTE: READ THIS - VERY IMPORTANT

Having medical supplies and medications and using those supplies correctly are two entirely different things. You should never take a prescription medication that has not been properly prescribed to you by a qualified medical professional. You should not take any medications that you are not familiar with, before consulting with your doctor or a qualified health care professional. Some medications, including antibiotics, can have severe side effects and, in some people, can cause more harm than good. The unsupervised use of any prescription medication is extremely dangerous and can potentially be fatal. Talk to your doctor and find out what medication(s) he/she recommends that you keep on hand for your particular situation, and also talk to your doctor about the risks of using any of those medications for your condition(s). Find out if you have any allergies to any medications (for example penicillin) and make sure that other members or your group or family know of your allergies in case you are injured and you can't communicate with your caregiver(s). <u>The information provided in this book is provided for illustration purposes only and does not provide, nor is it intended to provide, medical or any other type of professional advice to any reader. Any use of the information contained in this book shall be solely at the reader's risk.</u>

First Aid and Trauma Training

During *normal* times emergency medical services (EMS) are usually one phone call away. A call to a 911 operator will usually be adequate to dispatch an ambulance with emergency medical technicians and paramedics to your location. These emergency services usually provide pre-hospital acute care and transport. The main goal of all such emergency services is to provide immediate attention and treatment to those in need of urgent medical attention, with the goal of stabilizing and transporting the patient to the next point of definite care, usually a hospital or trauma center. During a WCS emergency medical services, or fire rescue may be delayed, or altogether absent. A routine call to a 911 operator may not be possible. And even if a 911 operator is available, there may not be sufficient units and personnel to dispatch, since the system may very well be overwhelmed by hundreds, maybe even thousands of emergency calls. EMS may even stop sending out units for fear of not being able to ensure the safety of its personnel.

There are many high quality first aid courses available nationwide. Classes are offered locally and online. There are also many books and publications available. I would strongly encourage you to invest some time and money and to take a quality course that offers first aid, CPR and other pre-hospital trauma care. These classes are incredibly valuable and some even include hands-on training. These courses are not offered for free, and sometimes require that you purchase books and other supplies, but they are well worth the money since you will gain a solid understanding of how to treat most life threatening injuries until you can get to a hospital. More importantly, you will get true *hands-on* experience, and the actual look and feel of doing it yourself; this is something that no book can provide. Free first aid courses are given at high schools or other charitable institutions, but they do not even begin to approach the level of training that you should be looking for.

Expirations Dates and Rotating Stores

When dealing with medications, people are usually concerned about expiration dates. This is understandable given the commonly held belief that most, if not all, mediations somehow become harmful if taken after the expiration date. Expiration dates on medications are mandated and represent the last date that the pharmaceutical manufacturer will guarantee that the product is at full potency. Understanding this, there is no reason to believe that a medication becomes harmful if used within a reasonable amount of time after the expiration date. Some studies have shown that over time a medication will start to lose its potency, but many commonly used antibiotics or other medications have been shown to remain effective for years after the expiration date.

When stockpiling medications for a WCS, you should store, rotate and consume in the same way you manage your food supplies. Don't just store and forget. Rotate the medications so that your supplies always have the freshest products available.

During a WCS medications may not be readily available or may become expensive beyond the reach of the average person. You may one day find yourself in just such a situation. Under normal, everyday circumstances, most people would never consider taking a medication that had expired, but during a WCS if nothing else is available, it's good to know that you have options.

<u>Please note that neither the author nor the publisher is in any way recommending that anyone take any expired medication. On the contrary, we strongly encourage readers to consult with their doctor, or other qualified health care professionals, before taking any medication, prescription or otherwise.</u>

Maintain Dental Health

Oral health is more important than most people realize. Problems in the mouth can affect the rest of the body. Poor dental and gum health can lead to severe complications, infections, and a decline in overall health. Researchers have shown links between poor oral health and an unhealthy body. During a crisis, is probably the worse time to have to deal with tooth aches, cavities, tooth abscess, infected gums; or a multitude of other oral conditions that can seriously affect your ability to eat, and your overall health. Brushing, flossing and visiting a dentist regularly for check-ups and cleanings will go a long way to help you avoid dental problems and complications. If you have any dental/oral issues, get them resolved now. And make sure to store sufficient quantities of floss, toothpaste, toothbrushes and mouthwash.

Vaccinations and Immunizations

Vaccinations and immunizations help us avoid preventable diseases, and help us stay healthy. Although this is an area of considerable debate, many health professionals agree that the positive usually outweighs the negative. Consult with your doctor and decide for yourself, but if you are considering getting vaccinated the Centers for Disease Control and Prevention website (www.cdc.gov/vaccines) provides information, schedules and recommendations for vaccinations and immunizations for the general public; this is a good place to start. During a WCS, when you are clearing rubble from around your home, and you get cut by a rusty piece of metal, that may not be the best time to start thinking about whether you have already gotten the recommended tetanus shot. Consider your options, discuss these options with your doctor and stay current on all the vaccines and immunizations well in advance of any crisis.

6: Personal Security, Self-Defense and Situational Awareness–It's Your Life...

"Though defensive violence will always be 'a sad necessity' in the eyes of men of principle, it would be still more unfortunate if wrongdoers should dominate just men."
-Saint Augustine

In This Chapter:

- Personal security and self-defense is, and always should be, the number one priority during any WCS.
- Self-defense using deadly force is a controversial topic, but one that must be confronted and resolved well in advance of any survival situation.
- Don't be a victim. Maintain the proper mindset and avoid becoming a target.
- During, and especially after, a WCS you should not count on the police or other first responders to protect you since they will probably be overwhelmed and severely understaffed.
- Keep a low profile and don't draw attention to yourself or your group.
- The best confrontation is the one that never happens. If you can flee the threat, get away as quickly and quietly as possible. Engage only if absolutely necessary.
- If fleeing is not an option, you should have a plan and be equipped to help stack the odds in your favor. If you must engage, make sure to do so on your own terms.
- You and your group/family should have the necessary discussions, and decide well in advance of any WCS, how you will respond to life threatening situations, and what level of

violence you are willing to use to protect yourself and your group.

- If you decide to use firearms for protection, know and follow the applicable laws – yes, even during a WCS.
- Select weapon(s) that suit the intended purpose, your personal preferences and that are comfortable to handle.
- Get proper training from qualified professionals. Take the time to learn the right way, from people who know what they're doing, and practice your new skills.
- With all rights come responsibilities, and it's your absolute, non-delegable obligation to handle and store your firearms in a safe and responsible manner.
- If within your means, set-up a small safe room for emergency situations.
- Conduct a realistic and practical self-defense assessment. Recognize and find a way to work around your self-defense limitations.

A Time to Decide

Self-defense and personal security is, and always should be, the number one priority during any survival situation. A healthy person can usually live for three days without water, and three weeks without food; but food and water very quickly become irrelevant when your life is in immediate danger. At that moment, your choices are very limited – flee, fight or face the risk of serious injury or even death. Assuming that most of us would never choose the third option, this chapter will focus on the first two.

While most reasonable people would prefer to never have to use deadly force against another human being, even in self defense, the vast majority of reasonable, rational people stand prepared to do so if it was the only way to protect themselves and their family. When confronted by a threat that is bigger, stronger and who is willing to use any level of violence to take whatever they want, you will need to be able to adequately and effectively defend yourself. If that moment comes, and most people hope it never will, you should have a clearly defined plan to defend yourself and others in your group; and you should be ready, willing and able to carry out that plan. I know this sounds harsh, but the subject of self-defense is a reality that way too many people ignore, until it's too late.

People are uncomfortable with this topic, and they would rather think that nothing bad will ever happen to them. And if something bad does happen, they hope that there will be others around to help; or that the police will arrive in time to protect them. If this is a topic that troubles you, rest assured - you are not alone. Self-defense is a tough topic for many people. Most of us have great difficulty with the thought of seriously injuring or killing another person. As a society we don't want it to be easy to take a life. But, it's a reality that you may one day have to face – ignoring it will not make it go away. Compared to this, the remainder of your survival planning will seem like a *cakewalk*.

Personal Security

Personal protection and self-defense are topics that many people rarely think about, or discuss openly. And when they do, it's usually not a very comfortable topic of conversation, especially if the conversation involves firearms. Nonetheless, if you value your life, it's a topic that deserves your careful thought, consideration, and clear discussions between you and your group members. This is one of those topics that require some level of agreement. Now is the best time to think about it, to discuss it openly, and to plan accordingly. To be as effective as possible, self-defense preparations require time, training and planning. Once the threat is upon you, it's way too late to start considering self-defense options. Coordinated action and proper training will increase your chances for survival in the aftermath of a WCS. If in the *thick of things* something should happen, you and your group should all be in agreement as to how you will address the threat. If there are people in your group that are not *in agreement*, they will be your *weak link*. This is something that you need to know and consider sooner rather than later - for your safety and for theirs.

As civilized members of society, we usually try to do everything possible to avoid violence, even in self-defense. This is one of those rules of legal and *moral* conduct that we're all expected to follow, and the majority of us do. We try to defuse potentially violent situations until help arrives, or we try to get away from those situations that we suspect may cause harm to us or others. This is not a bad thing; violence should be avoided when there are other available options. And in today's environment, even violence committed in justifiable self-defense situations can cause a person to be arrested, charged and tried – sometimes even convicted. You, the intended victim, may eventually prevail and win your case, but not before spending many years fighting the charges, tens of thousands of dollars on legal fees, and having your life, and peace of mind, ruined. You might even have to worry about retaliation from the criminal's confederates. Knowing this, most people are very reluctant to act to protect themselves, even when doing so would be fully rational, and legally permissible. Criminals know this and they are counting on it. They don't care about the law, or how their actions may be perceived. They don't even care if they harm innocents as they pursue their selfish ends. To them, you are not a human being, you are merely an object to be used as they see fit.

Typical criminals have a predator mentality, and are looking for targets of opportunity. If you don't give them an opportunity, they will move along until someone does. They certainly don't want to risk injury, arrest or possibly even death; they want a quick and easy target. That target of opportunity should never be you, or any member of your group. During the confusion and panic of a crisis, criminals will quickly seize the opportunity to do what they do best - prey on victims.

What You Should Expect

Violent crime is a global concern and it can occur to anyone at anytime; as such, you should always be aware of your surroundings and prepared for the *unexpected*. During and after a WCS the issue of self-defense becomes extremely important. After any major disaster, the police, and other first responders, will be forced to confront demands that will far exceed their capabilities. To make matters worse, over the last few years many police departments have seen severe budget cuts and layoffs. The resulting cutbacks have left many departments seriously underfunded and understaffed. Prior to the cuts, many police departments were already having difficulty keeping up with the *everyday* demands of their community. How will these down-sized departments possibly keep up in the aftermath of a major crisis?

Consider some of the worse crime-ridden cities. Even though some of these places are believed to be among the most dangerous in the country, budget cuts have forced massive police layoffs. Regardless of the eventual outcome, criminals in and around these municipalities, must be *jumping for joy*; this is an urban failure on a massive scale. Imagine being a law-abiding resident of one of these localities and calling the police for some emergency only to find out that there are no units available to respond to your call – you're essentially on your own. Imagine such a scenario during or after a WCS.

It's important to remember that it's not just the actual police officers; all first responders, rely on a massive infrastructure of operators, dispatchers, support and administrative staff to keep the emergency response systems and related functions operational. What happens when these folks can't or won't go to work? If the roads are blocked, or if the situation is too dangerous for commuting, how many 911 operators and support staff do you think will be willing to leave their families, and the relative safety of their homes to go to work? I'm guessing not many; and as conditions deteriorate even fewer still. Remember this is all playing out in an environment that is already plagued with low-moral and overall job dissatisfaction due to serious pay-cuts, layoffs and dangerous working conditions.

During and after a WCS, police response times may be stretched from minutes to hours or even days. Sadly, if your phone is not working, or if the 911 system is overwhelmed or somehow compromised, help may never arrive. Phones are great for calling for help, and for some strange reason, people take great comfort in the fact that they have a phone – sadly a phone itself will never protect anyone. Even under the best of circumstance, calling for help has some very serious time limitations, time

you may not have. After a WCS, calling for help and actually getting
that help will be two entirely different things.

After a WCS, many people may find that they are on their own.
Sadly, many criminals will be quick to take advantage of the situation. After all the stores are looted and destroyed, criminals will turn
their attention to you, and others like you. Under those circumstances
most people may only be able to keep what they can defend; this will
include food, water, and maybe even their very life. This may be a very
disturbing thought, especially to people who have never had to think
this way. However, just because it's a difficult topic doesn't mean you
should not recognize and consider its importance in your survival plan.

In troubled times six skills will be very valuable, and may help
to keep you alive:

1. Your ability to successfully avoid confrontations, violent or
    otherwise.
2. Your ability to evaluate situations quickly and accurately
    and decide on appropriate responses.
3. Your ability to quickly and effectively recognize dangerous
    situations and people, and to respond quickly and decisively.
4. Your ability to promptly shift between different levels of
    awareness and alertness. (More on this later.)
5. Your ability to act rapidly, definitively and without
    hesitation.
6. Your ability to call upon the needed physical strength, en-
    durance, self-defense skills and the proper tools to protect
    yourself and your family.

Having and employing these skills will help keep you and your
family alive and well during any WCS. Not developing an understanding of these six skills and how they will impact your situation will
very quickly increase the odds of you becoming a victim. This way
of thinking should become natural and automatic. (By the way, these

skills are important not just during a WCS, but even during *normal* times.)

Don't Become a Victim

By and large, most people stumble around blissfully going about their daily routines, mostly unaware of their surroundings, and frequently preoccupied with random thoughts. Few people, if any, ever give personal security more than a passing thought, and fewer still are even remotely aware of their immediate surroundings. When a threat materializes and hits them squarely in the face, they react with total shock and surprise. *He just came out of nowhere!*

Under these high stress conditions, most people are immediately paralyzed with fear. Some manage to pull themselves together long enough to call the police. Given the distracted mental and unfit physical state of the majority of the U.S. population, it's not surprising that most people are woefully unprepared, to do anything other than dial 911, and wait for whatever help may come and at whatever time it may arrive.

The typical victim mentality is as follows: *I'm a good person, I mind my own business and I don't bother anybody. Why would someone want to hurt me or my family?* The simple truth is that it's not about you. You were just in the wrong place at the wrong time, and unfortunately you became a target of opportunity. Unknown to most people, their attitude and body language are constantly broadcasting more information to the world around them than they could ever have imagined.

If a person looks weak, unaware, helpless, and distracted they might as well put a large neon sign over their head saying "Come and Get Me!" Criminals don't care about you, your family or any rules of legal or moral conduct. They have a very simple agenda – to satisfy their own selfish needs/wants in the easiest and fastest way possible. But, just by increasing your awareness of your surroundings; and changing the image that you project to others, can have a dramatic impact on lowering your chances of becoming a victim. In other words, even just recognizing the potential threats that exist around you and re-adjusting your behavior accordingly, may one day help save your life.

Here is a very common example:

Two people are walking out of a large store late at night. (Let's call them person "A" and "B"). Both individuals are loaded down with heavy bags and both must walk to their cars that are parked about 50 yards away from the store entrance. Both "A" and "B" are tired, hungry and can't wait to get home after a long day. In other words they are stressed, and possibly inattentive.

Person "A" walks out into the darkness, oblivious and preoccupied by random thoughts. Despite carrying an uncomfortably heavy load, "A" still manages to hold a cell phone conversation with a friend complaining about all the day's events. "A" can't remember where the car is parked since "A" was also distracted when parking the car hours earlier. "A" is not looking around, scanning the parking lot or evaluating the surroundings. "A" has not even thought about the possibility of being attacked, and naturally would be taken completely by surprised by any such event, and would be frozen in shock having no idea how to respond. "A" is unwittingly doing all the rights things to become a victim, to invite an attack, and serious injury or maybe even death.

Person "B" on the other hand came into the parking lot much earlier in the day, anticipating that it would probably be dark by the time "B" was done shopping, and wisely parked their car under a large street light; in an area with high visibility and heavy pedestrian traffic. Even before exiting the building "B" performs a visual scan of the parking lot and the surrounding areas. "B" wisely defers phone calls, texts or other distractions for a later time, and instead walks cautiously and with purpose towards the car, keys in hand. "B" is not anticipating any problems, but is alert and vigilant to any activity that may signal danger. At the first sign of anything that seems *out-of-place*, or suspicious, "B" is prepared to automatically and quickly move to the next level of awareness. Person "B" has also visualized a number of possible scenarios and carefully thought about and decided in advance on appropriate responses. By thinking about these things and planning ahead "B" has taken a substantial degree of control over any such circumstances, should they occur.

By the way, "B" also keeps a careful eye out for distracted drivers. "B" knows that not all potential threats are intentional; some threats come from well-meaning people that are just inattentive, careless, and irresponsible.

Person "B" has a mindset of awareness and precaution, and will not make an easy target. "B" is alert, aware of the surroundings, is constantly assessing the environment, has planned ahead, is prepared for the unexpected, and refuses to be a victim, and the body language confirms this. Person "A" on the other hand has a *bulls eye* painted on their back, and is vulnerable to just about any unfortunate event, intentional or otherwise. Do you see the difference?

This is a made-up scenario, but it happens every day. The facts and circumstances are common, can be applied to just about any situation. I picked this example because most of us can relate to the situation. But we could have just as easily used an example about being caught in the aftermath of a natural disaster, walking to your car in a large parking lot of a high-rise building, or having to make your way home after a major power outage, storm or flood takes out the mass transit system in your community. The same principles apply to all these situations. How you conduct yourself and how aware you are of the environment around you will, in large part, determine how you are perceived by those who would do you harm, given the opportunity.

Avoidance - The First Line of Defense

You may not realize it, but every single day you make thousands of decisions. Some of little important, other decisions can make the difference between life and death — *to save time on my drive to work should I take a short-cut through a dangerous neighborhood?*

Reasonable people know that it's much better to avoid a problem than to deal with the consequences afterwards. As in our example above, a sensible person would choose to get up earlier and to take the safer route to work, avoiding obvious dangers. Is the safer route a guarantee of personal safety? Absolutely not! In fact, I would encourage you to be on alert regardless of where you might happen to be, since anything can happen to anyone regardless of where they are. But, to knowingly put oneself in a dangerous situation and naively hope that nothing bad happens is foolish and irresponsible. Thinking ahead, anticipating potential problems and taking reasonable steps to avoid those situation; it's a way of life for some, not so much for others.

During and after a WCS, this way of thinking becomes even more significant, since the stakes will be much higher. When the world around you is turned upside down, and people are hysterical, running around as if they lost their minds, the best defense, should always be to stay out of sight and to keep a very low profile. During those difficult moments there is no disputing that old saying about an ounce of prevention being worth a pound of cure. Avoiding problems and unnecessary confrontations may help save your life. You should remember that, during a WCS, it's not your job to go outside and *fix* the problem(s). The magnitude of any such problems will be beyond the capacity of any one person. Your job is to deal with and manage the effects of the situation within your own home, and how it may affect you and your family. When it's feasible, avoidance is usually the best and safest option.

If things get really bad, here are some strategies to help you keep a low profile:

1. If you decide to stay put, do exactly that - stay put! Remain inside your home and don't go outside, unless absolutely necessary. Don't walk around the neighborhood trying to find out what news your neighbors may have heard – they probably know less than you do. Stay inside and keep your family away from windows and doors.

2. No interaction is best. If you must engage others, keep all interactions brief. The less people know about you, where you are, what supplies you have and the status of your overall situation, the better.

3. Maintain operational security. Don't bring anyone into your home. If you must engage, do it outside. Remember, desperate people do desperate things. Don't test your luck with anybody. If you do bring a known person into your home, make sure they understand and agree to abide by your rules. Even during normal times it's never a good idea to bring a stranger into your home; after a WCS it should be completely out of the question.

4. Keep your supplies out of sight. Don't pile up your supplies in the living room next to a window, or by an open door. This may seem obvious to most, but you may be surprised by how many people don't consider it necessary to take these types of precautions.

5. Only run generators when absolutely necessary and never in plain sight. The noise from a generator will announce your presence to all for miles. Always try to mask the location of any outdoor equipment, such as a generator. You can deflect some of the generator's noise away from your house, by using a few well placed pieces of plywood. Cut and paint/stain (to serve as camouflage) the plywood pieces in advance. It's not 100%, but it will help.

6. Avoid any sort of lights at night. If the power is out, using lights at night will announce to the world that you have supplies; or at least will qualify you as a target of interest. Have a few flashlights with red lenses to conserve night vision and use them sparingly. Try to complete all tasks during daylight hours, at night just lay low and stay quiet.

7. Do not cook. During a WCS is not the time to fire-up the BBQ grill or to set-up that outside kitchen. The smell of food carries for long distances and once you are detected it will put a *bull's-eye* directly on you and your home. If you planned properly, you should have stored prepared foods that require no cooking and that can be eaten at room

temperature using nothing more than a can opener and a spoon. (More on this in Chapter 4.)

8. Keep all exterior doors, windows and gates closed and locked. Make sure that all the members of your group do the same. It just takes one careless act to compromise the security of the entire group.

9. Keep windows, shades and curtains closed.

10. Black-out all outward facing windows, or use a thick, matte black material to cover the inside of all windows, and doors that have glass panels. The idea is to avoid any actions that may draw attention to you or your home.

11. Don't engage strangers, no matter how pathetic they may seem. Bad guys don't always look the part, and they can sometimes be very convincing. That harmless looking person asking for a glass of water may be part of a much larger group trying to figure out which homes are worth hitting and which are not. Once you become a target – it's only a matter of time.

12. Invest in some extra supplies and share with your neighbors. Keep a separate stash of canned/boxed food and some plastic bottles filled with water to share. Helping to feed your neighbors is a good thing; cooperation and sharing is always better than armed confrontations. Just don't compromise your security. Keep your *real* stash well hidden and secured, preferably in several different locations throughout your home. You should never access your supplies in the presence of anyone outside your immediate group. This is not about being selfish, it's about survival. Your number one priority has to be you and your family/group. Revealing what you have to anyone, can put you and yours, at great risk. Not only because someone may want to take what you have, but because they may also decide to hurt you in the process. During a crisis even a simple injury can become life threatening.

13.   In extreme circumstances, if you and your supplies are discovered, and aggressors do come, a strong show of force may send them away temporarily. But it's important to remember, while they may initially go after easier targets, they will keep you in mind, and once all the easy target have been taken, they will come back, this time better prepared and better armed.

Note: If you stay out of sight, and you still get noticed you will need to make some important decisions. Do you stay, or do you go? Do you make a stand? Do you have the means to defend your location and are your people properly trained and equipped? And finally, do you even have a defensible position and are you willing to pay the potential costs? None of these questions will be easy to answer and much will depend on how well you have prepared.

When avoidance is not an option, and fleeing is not an option and you need to defend yourself, then your plan should be designed to help you stack the odds in your favor as much as possible. A well thought out plan should allow you to make the best use of the resources at your disposal, and to use force-multipliers when available. Note: A *force multiplier* is a capability or technology that when properly used significantly increases the potential of the particular force used and enhances the probability of success. For example a chain saw is a force multiplier of sorts, since it allow one person to cut as much wood as quickly as a much larger group of people working with hand saws. A small group of special forces operatives can often engage and overpower large groups of enemy forces by using *force multipliers* such as special equipment, advanced technology, and of course superior training and real-time intelligence.

If you are forced into a self-defense situation you will want to end the hostilities quickly; to do so you will need to strike hard, fast and with over whelming force. Once you are attacked there can be no hesitation. Playing defense never won a battle, and by itself it's not enough; if your opponent is on the attack and all you are doing is defending, it's only a matter of time before one of his attacks is successful. Remember, he only needs to be successful, or lucky, once.

Your goal is to neutralize the threat and to end the fight quickly. The longer the struggle goes on the higher your risk of serious injury or death. In a WCS even a minor injury can quickly become complicated and life threatening. Knowing this you'll want to avoid even the possibility of injury. Plan ahead accordingly, and avoid unnecessary risks. Once you go down this road, half measures are just not possible, especially if you want to live.

Note: In the aftermath of a crisis there may be a period of time during which there has not been a total collapse situation, or there have been some efforts at restoring some semblance of order, but things are not quite "normal". Under those circumstances we may still need to get up each morning and go about our business, of work, school, etc. These may actually be more dangerous times than when we remain at home and stay out of sight, since we are exposing ourselves to unknown dangers and hazards, but we are still expected to function as usual. There may be intermittent electrical power, and police, fire fighters and other public services may be functioning at limited capacity. At such times the risks are many and your options may be few.

Self Defense and Firearms

When a threat comes at you, it will come fast, hard, and without any warning. At that moment you may not have time to flee. For most of us, how we respond to a potentially life-threatening threat will be determined by our conditioning, moral convictions, self-defense philosophy, training, our level of preparedness, and what weapons we have at our disposal.

If you are willing to defend yourself, or your family, you must make sure that you, and your family, are mentally and physically prepared for that moment. If you are not willing to defend yourself then you must also be prepared, since there is a very real possibility that you might die at the hands of a violent attacker. If this happens, your surviving family members will need to fend for themselves.

Protecting yourself and your family is a job that can best be accomplished by a well armed individual, preferably more than one individual. That means that unless you have, and know how to use firearms, you will probably be at a serious disadvantage. Few weapons level the playing field like a firearm. In a fight, size, weight, strength and gender are all relevant factors. But, if you can aim, pull a trigger and hit your target; a ninety-eight pound female can be just as effective as a six foot tall man at double the weight. Pepper spray, mace, stun guns and other less lethal options may sound viable in theory, but they will usually lack the power/force necessary to stop a determined, armed assailant, or multiple armed assailants. Worse yet, if your attackers get discouraged and go away after a good dose of pepper spray, they will most likely be back. And next time they will be better armed and ready to use whatever force is necessary to take you down – and it probably won't be with pepper spray.

If and when the time comes to defend yourself with a firearm, you must make sure that you have the proper training and the proper equipment. Picking up a gun and shooting it may sound easy, but it's not. Under extreme duress even simple motor skills become exceedingly difficult to carry out. You will not only need to know what to do, but you will need to be able to do it under extremely stressful situations.

If you are planning on scaring people away by showing them your gun, forget about it. Unlike the movies, attackers don't usually run and hide at the sight of a gun. It is also highly unlikely that you will be able to shoot the gun out of an attacker's hand, or injure the bad guy in the leg like in the old westerns. Proper training will dictate how and where you place your shots, and why. Using your firearm as you've seen actors do in the movies will get you killed. The movies are entertainment, and everything done in the movies is performed to *look good*, not to be effective or to work in real life.

The Armed Self-Defense Debate

When a person takes the life of an attacker, in self defense, they are usually judged very harshly by the media and society at large. I don't expect that this will change any time soon; even after a WCS.

From the comfort and security of their living room couch, people with little to no knowledge of the actual facts assume that there must have been some other, non-violent, way to have handled the situation, to have avoided the loss of life. The unfortunate incident usually becomes a referendum on the use of deadly force, and the ownership of firearms, with little or no attention paid to the fact that the person that was shot and/or killed was a criminal trying to kill or cause serious bodily injury to the real victim, who did nothing to provoke the attack.

It's very easy to criticize after-the-fact, especially if none of those passing judgment were actually there when the events played out. I always wonder if these *Monday Morning Quarterbacks* would have handled it any differently if they had been the ones attacked. Maybe they would have defused the situation by appealing to the attacker's sense of basic human kindness and morality. Or maybe they would have surrendered their life to the attacker just to avoid using any violence. Sounds ridiculous, doesn't it? Remember your first choice will usually be to flee, if that option is available to you.

Deadly force with a firearm is a politically charged topic, with passionate opinions on all sides. Some folks strongly believe that no one, expect law enforcement should ever have access to any firearms – and they make no exceptions for self defense. On the other extreme there are folks who advocate for a fully armed citizenry with absolutely no restrictions whatsoever. This is a debate as contentious as religion, politics, abortion, and birth control and one not likely to be resolved anytime soon. This ridiculous and illogical debate will no doubt continue for many years to come. It's an argument that's largely about opinions, and has very little to do with fact or reality. We will skip the debate…

One very straightforward and practical way to look at all this is as follows: subject to the applicable state and federal laws, you may want to consider every possible legal option to help you defend yourself, and your family against violent attackers. As long as there are guns, and other deadly weapons that criminals can use against you, and your family, why would you ever choose to put yourself at any sort of disadvantage? While there are many people who will vehemently disagree with this logic, you alone are responsible for the health and welfare of your family, and you should take that responsibility very seriously. The day may come when whatever preparations you have made for self-defense, will be the only thing standing between you and an armed attacker(s). The opinions of the misinformed and the ill advised will do you little good, and will bring you little comfort the day you find yourself staring down the barrel of a loaded gun. If at that moment you are caught empty handed and unprepared, you and your family will probably face and suffer the consequences all on your own. Critics and hypocrites are always in attendance to provide unsolicited advice and opinions, they're rarely, if ever, present when it really matters.

The folks who see no need to arm themselves mistakenly believe that the police will always be there, armed and ready, to protect them and their family. This is an unrealistic belief, but one that they embrace passionately. I see no need to argue or debate the issue with those who disagree, the law says what the law says. And if the law in your jurisdiction allows you to be armed to defend yourself, the options seem pretty obvious. And if nothing else it's your decision, not anyone else's. I am always very skeptical and uncomfortable with people who have no difficulty imposing their opinions, beliefs and convictions on others.

You should remember that even though your first choice should be to avoid potentially violent confrontations, any halfway decent survival plan will require you to consider your self-defense options well in advance, and to include a strong self-defense component as part of the overall plan. To that end you should consider every possible legal option available to you.

Gun Ownership and Training

All too often people are quick to claim their rights, although few are ever as eager to acknowledge or accept the responsibilities that come along with those rights. Owning a gun is not only a right, but also a huge responsibility. I strongly encourage anyone who owns a gun, or who is considering buying one, to become familiar with all the applicable laws on the ownership, storage and use of firearms in their jurisdiction, and to get proper training.

A gun is not good or evil, it's an inanimate object; it's a tool used for a specific purpose - nothing more, nothing less. And, as with any other tool, if you misuse it, you will probably end up unintentionally hurting yourself or someone else. There are many very good schools across the U.S. that can teach you marksmanship, proper gun handling skills, tactical skills, and techniques for using, maintaining, and storing your firearms. There are even schools/instructors that focus on specialized tactical firearms training, and close quarter battle scenarios.

Find a professional instructor that teaches in a way that suits your needs and your style. If you are comfortable, you will learn and retain more. A good firearms instructor will teach you many valuable skills that will allow you to use your firearms in the most effective way possible. Professional training will include marksmanship skills, gun handling skills and tactical skills. But learning a skill is not enough. Shooting well is a perishable skill. If you don't practice you will lose any advantage you may have gained in your training. To maintain your newly minted skills you will need, not only practice, but good quality practice. Once again, you will not only need to know what to do and how to do it, but you will need to be able to apply those skills at times of tremendous duress.

This is a book about urban survival, not about weapons, defensive tactics or shooting skills. The following information is intended to serve just as an introduction to get you thinking about the different options. If you are not an experienced, well trained shooter, you have a lot to learn. A weapon is a very big responsibility. And legally, morally and ethically you have many obligations that you must be ready, willing and able to accept before you decide to buy or use any firearm.

NOTE: make sure that you are familiar with the applicable state and federal gun laws in your jurisdiction; this is your responsibility. Ignorance will not excuse your actions. As a responsible gun owner you must know and fully understand the laws where you live, and the potential legal consequences of using your firearms for self-defense. A WCS only changes things for the criminals, law abiding people most always obey the law.

Additionally, you and you alone are responsible for storing and maintaining your weapons in a safe and secure location. Every year children, and some adults who have no business handling a firearm, find loaded, unsecured guns and can't resist the urge to *play* with them. When someone gets hurt or killed, the adult gun owners will usually be held legally responsible for any tragedies resulting from their care-less actions.

Choosing a Firearm

Choosing a firearm is a personal decision that should not be based on something you once heard a friend say, or on a review you read in a gun magazine, or worse yet - something you saw on TV. A firearm is a lifesaving piece of equipment and should be chosen with care. If you are new to shooting, you will need to research and experience many different types of firearms before you find the right one(s) for you. I encourage you to do your own research, talk to professions in the field, and most importantly get some hands-on experience with the different options. Take your time and learn the differences in quality, function-ality and effectiveness. There will of course be the issue of cost – for the firearms and the ammunition. As you would expect, you get what you pay for. But then again; how much is your life worth?

For some very practical reasons, some weapons will be better than others. Choosing the weapon(s) for home and personal self-defense is an important matter and should not be rushed. Many factors will influ-ence your decisions. Consider some of the following:

- Price and budget. Firearms are not inexpensive; ammuni-tion costs can also add up quickly. Doing your homework will help you in finding a balance between affordability and effectiveness.

- Sizes and configurations. The intended purpose of a firearm will in many instances help you in narrowing your choices. Is the weapon for home defense or for concealed carry? Larger weapons are usually easier to handle and shoot since they absorb some of the felt recoil. The smaller firearms are more difficult to control, but easier to conceal and carry. If the weapon is meant for home defense, size will not be so much of a consideration since concealment won't be an issue. Remember there is no one-size-fits-all weapon. Don't take anybody's word for it; test out the different options and judge for yourself.

- Caliber. The debate over caliber effectiveness and stopping power is endless. Some experts argue that size matters; others argue that shot placement matters more. Don't get caught up in the technical debate. The more powerful ammunition will make the gun more difficult to control. The smaller ammunition will have less recoil but may not be as effective as the larger caliber ammunition. Many self-defense experts recommend the 9mm round as a good compromise. The 9mm round is used by NATO forces and the U.S. military. It has been around for years and is relatively inexpensive compared to larger more powerful rounds. Remember that everything in life requires a tradeoff. You'll need to decide what you want, and what you are willing to give up, in order to get it. Test the different options for yourself, and you decide what works for you. Most experts do not recommend anything smaller than a 9mm round for self-defense.

- Firearm design has come a long way; many of the latest models are light, compact and offer lots of capacity and effective firepower. Don't overlook some of these newer options. When the Glock semi-automatic pistols first came out, few people understood that they were actually seeing the future of firearms in the making. Today the .40 caliber

Glock is the most commonly issued law enforcement pistol, and many manufactures now offer Glock style pistols.

- Pick a weapon that is easy to train with and easy to learn to use. If you don't like it, you won't practice and you won't shoot it well.
- Select a weapon that is easy to take apart, clean and maintain. Firearms require regular cleaning and maintenance to keep them functioning safely and properly. Dirty guns can be unsafe, and are more likely to fail when you need them the most.
- Select a weapon that is easy to handle, and that offers a wide selection of grip sizes, configurations, parts and accessories. One size should never fit all.
- Select a weapon that is easy to load and reload. Preloaded magazines and proper training will afford you some very fast reloading options on these types of weapons. This is especially important if you live in a state that restricts magazine capacity.
- Depending on where you live, magazines are available that can hold anywhere from 8 to 30 rounds for most semi-auto pistols and rifles. These high capacity magazines may be illegal in some states, check before you buy.
- Wide choice of makers, calibers, and finishes for any budget.
- Wide choice of accessories including lights, lasers, electronic sights.
- Consider a firearm for which parts will be easy to find. Or better yet buy and store extra parts for when the need arises.

Consider all the options. You may want to become proficient on various weapon systems, since no one weapon is appropriate for every situation. There are many who consider the 12-gauge shotgun loaded with 00 buck to be the ultimate home self-defense weapon. Some people love the shotgun, but others are scared off by the shotgun's notorious recoil – it kicks hard when fired. Some people may prefer something a bit more manageable. Also, a shotgun may work for you inside your home, but it's very difficult to walk around with a shotgun. If you plan on ever leaving the house and need to be adequately armed, a pistol will probably be the only option. A pistol straps to your waist, is far more comfortable and a lot easier to conceal especially in warmer climates. Remember during and after a WCS you may still have to go out, albeit in a far more cautious manner. Carrying a rifle or shotgun in those circumstances may not be practical or even possible. Again, there is no one weapon to fit all circumstances and needs.

There are of course many good options and every year new products come to market. Keep an open mind and look for alternatives. In the meantime, here are some options for you to consider. At the end of the day it's your decision; what works for one person may not work for others. Take your time and make sure you do your *homework* before spending your hard-earned cash.

Shotgun for Home Defense

The 12-gauge pump action shotgun is probably the most recognized and commonly used home defense firearm. It is both feared and respected. When used properly, and with the correct ammunition, it can be a very effective home defense tool. Here are some points to consider.

The pros:
- The pump action shotgun has been around for many years and has been used extensively by our troops in battle, and on the streets by law enforcement.
- At close range the 12-gauge shotgun is extremely powerful and can do a lot of damage. Pulling the trigger of a shotgun is serious stuff.
- The three most common shotgun shells are:

o   00 Buck shot – Buck shot is the most commonly used ammunition for self defense. Very effective stopping power. It will reduce, but not eliminate over-penetration of adjoining structures, especially in urban environments where people live in very close proximity to one another, and over-penetration is a very real concern.

o   Bird shot – Bird shot can also be used for self defense. It's not as effective as 00 buckshot, but offers additional protection against over-penetration in close quarters.

o   The slug – Slugs are not generally recommended for indoor urban use because of their power and over-penetration. Slugs will easily go through most interior walls, interior and exterior doors and exterior walls. They will also go through car doors and windshields. Slugs are also far more accurate and effective at longer distances than bird shot or 00 buck shot.

- Less lethal ammunition is now also available for use in shotguns. In most instances less lethal ammunition will hurt, but not kill. You can expect many more choices of less lethal ammunition in the future.
- The shotgun offers a very stable shooting platform with four points of contact – the butt of the stock on the upper pectoral, both hands (dominant & support) and the cheek weld. This additional stability gives the shooter more control and allows for faster follow-up shots.
- Modern pump shotguns are extremely reliable, durable and don't often malfunction.
- Modern pump shotguns accept and fire just about any brand of ammunition you put into them. They are not picky when it comes to your choice of ammunition.
- Shotguns are usually more affordable than other rifles.

- There are lots of manufacturers at many different price points.
- Shotguns are also offered in semi-automatic – no need to pump.
- Many manufacturers are now offering lots of options, accessories and configurations. Lights, lasers, slings, stocks, grips, etc.
- Recent advances in shotgun technology have increased effectiveness, flexibility and the durability of materials used.

The Cons:
- A shotgun's recoil is not for the faint hearted. A 12-gauge shotgun will kick like an angry mule. Heavy recoil makes the shotgun more difficult to control and to shoot accurately. Some ammunition manufactures offer low-recoil tactical ammunition. But even with reduced-recoil ammunition, recoil can still be an issue for smaller shooters.
- Over penetration can be a big concern especially in a home with sheetrock walls or an urban environment, with other structures in close proximity.
- Becoming proficient with the shotgun requires more extensive training and practice, than other firearm options.
- Requires more frequent reloads. Doesn't compare favorably with the 30 round magazine of a 5.56 rifle.
- The commonly held misconception that it is impossible to miss with a shotgun; is just that – a misconception. A shotgun must still be aimed.

AR-15 (M4 style) Carbine for Home Defense

The AR/M4 style (in 5.56/.223) rifle/carbine is a formidable option for home defense. It's accurate, lethal and easier to learn to use and maintain than comparable weapon systems.

The Pros:

- The AR platform has been around for years and has literally proven itself, all around the world, on battlefields and on the streets by law enforcement agencies.
- The 5.56 round is powerful and can do a lot of damage.
- A rifle built to use the 5.56 round can use the less powerful and less expensive .223 round. Conversely, a rifle built for the .223 should not be used with the more powerful 5.56 round. The .223 round is often used for target practice or for training, but can also be very effective for self defense.
- The 5.56 and .223 ammunition is plentiful, easy to obtain and relatively inexpensive.
- It's relatively easy to use – very little felt recoil. It doesn't kick you like a shotgun, allowing for better shot placement, accuracy and quicker follow-up shots.
- Lots of manufacturers offer many different configurations and price points.
- Lots of available options and aftermarket configurations. Lights, lasers, optics, slings, stocks, grips, magazines, other accessories, etc.
- Lots of readily available replacement parts.
- Very high capacity magazines available. Depending in what State you live you can buy magazines that can hold anywhere from 10 to 30 rounds, some are even larger.

The Cons:

- Modern M4 style carbines can be expensive. Prices start at around $800.00 and go up from there.
- Accessories can quickly add up and more than double the original purchase price.
- The 5.56 and .223 rounds have been criticized as not being powerful enough. (You can also now get a M4 style carbine chambered for larger more powerful ammunition.)
- Loaded up with accessories the rifle can get heavy.

The M4 style carbines are a favorite self-defense choice among many weapons experts and firearms instructors. If you are ever faced with a home invasion or are somehow up against multiple armed attackers, an M4 style carbine configured with optics, a flashlight and a few extra magazines makes for a formidable self-defense set-up. The carbine has lots of loyal fans, and when properly configured can act as a *force multiplier* allowing one person to engage and deal with multiple threats in a very effective manner.

Handguns for Home Defense

Sometimes a rifle is not an option. Other times, even though you started out with the rifle as your primary weapon, it was somehow taken out of the fight by a jam or a malfunction. It's at these times that a semi-automatic pistol chambered in 9mm is an excellent back-up option for home defense. It's lightweight, maneuverable, deadly accurate at close range, easy to learn to use, and with today's modern designs you can fire many rounds of ammunition before a reload is necessary. There are some who will argue that the 9mm round is less than desirable for self-defense since it lacks the stopping power of larger rounds, such as the 40mm and/or the .45 ACP. That may be true, but to many, modern 9mm self-defense ammunition represents a reasonable compromise, delivering respectable stopping power but with much lower recoil than larger, more powerful ammunition. The 9mm rounds are also more affordable compared to the 40mm or the .45 ACP. (But, if you want to step it up to a larger, more powerful caliber the 40mm is an excellent choice.)

The Pros:
- The 9mm pistol round has been around for years and has proven itself in battle. Currently used by NATO forces and the U.S. Military.
- Most 9mm pistols have a relatively easy learning curve.
- The 9mm is a powerful round that can do a lot of damage, while maintaining a balance between stopping power and felt recoil.

- Modern 9mm self-defense ammunition is highly effective.
- Relatively easy to use, shoot, clean and maintain. Recoil is manageable.
- Lots of manufacturers at many different and affordable price points.
- Lots of options and configurations. Lights, sights, lasers, grips, etc.
- Very high capacity magazines. Depending in what State you live you can buy magazines that can hold anywhere from 10 to 30 rounds.
- Fast and easy reloads.
- Fast and easy procedures to clear jams and mis-fed ammunition.
- Conceal ability allows the 9mm pistol to also be used as a concealed carry self-defense firearm where permitted by law, and with the proper permits.
- Good back-up and support weapon in the event of a primary weapon malfunction or jam.

The Cons:
- The pistol will never be as powerful or as effective as a shotgun or an AR-15 or M4 style carbine.

Again, there is no such thing as a one-size-fits-all weapon —each has a purpose. At the end of the day when all the "experts" have given their opinion, the only thing that matters is what you want and what works for you.

Self Defense – Hand-to-Hand

For obvious reasons, going *hand-to-hand* with an attacker should never be your first choice. Unless you are a trained fighter, or a martial arts expert, fighting with just your hands can be very hazardous to your health. In fact, the number one rule in hand-to-hand fighting should be – don't do it. All it takes is one lucky blow, and you can be out of the fight and seriously hurt. Having said that, there are certain skills, techniques and knowledge that will help you get out of a bind if you are attacked and caught by surprise, or if you are not near any potential weapons. In these situations your main goal should always be to disable the attacker and to give yourself enough time to get away.

1.   Take immediate and decisive action to stop the attack – Take whatever advantages you are given. Whether it's an opportunity to strike at the attacker's eyes, groin, throat or any other vulnerable area – take it. Don't be squeamish; remember you're in a fight for your life. Strike at your attacker's weak points and keep striking until he goes down. Here is a list of the most vulnerable body parts.

   a.   **Testicles/Groin**: a strong kick or knee to the groin is a powerful motivator. If a kick or knee is not possible, grab the groin, twist and pull down with all your might.

   b.   **Eyes**: Applying even a small amount of pressure to the eyes with your thumbs will cause tremendous pain and temporarily blindness.

   c.   **Ears**: Cup your hands and clap your open palms over both ears. This will usually cause the ear drum to rupture and quite possibly render the attacker unconscious.

   d.   **Nose**: A sharp, well placed blow to the bottom of the nose, using the heal of your palm, can be devastating.

   e.   **Throat**: If an attacker can't breathe, he can't pursue you. A blow to the throat can cause severe damage to the airway. While he's catching his breath, you can be running as fast as your legs will take you.

   f.   **Knees**: A sharp kick to the front or either side of the knee can quickly take an attacker to the ground.

2.   Disable the attacker so that he can't come after you again – Don't linger, but also make sure that you won't be pursued.

If you fail to disable the attacker, he will get up and come at you again, and now he's angry.

3.   Get away as quickly as possible – Call the police or get help.

Sounds simple? It's not. When you are attacked, fear and panic can overwhelm you and cause a sort of paralysis that can stop you dead in your tracks. To overcome this you will need knowledge, a plan, and some simple techniques. Avoiding the confrontation is even better. But if you are attacked, and avoidance is not an option, your overall success depends on three principles:

1.   Situational Awareness, always be mindful of your surroundings. Never get too comfortable, even in familiar surroundings.

2.   Control your fear and your emotions – turn your fear into a motivator for forceful and decisive action. Get angry and turn that anger into forceful action.

3.   Target key spots - Be aware of the body's weaknesses and how you can use those weaknesses to your advantage. (See Above)

I would serious encourage anyone interested in self-defense to get proper training. Reading about some techniques or watching some videos on-line may provide some perspective, but none of these are acceptable substitutes for proper training. To be truly effective, you must learn what works, and then practice it until it becomes second nature. And it's important to remember, it's not enough to know what to do, you must be able to do it under tremendously stressful situations.

The Home Invasion

A home invasion is one of the most frightening and dangerous crimes that can occur to a family - a nightmare come true. It's the act of illegally entering a private dwelling, by force or deception, with the intent of committing crimes against the occupants. Some of these crimes include robbery, rape, assault, murder or kidnapping. We have all seen the news stories; a typical home invasion does not usually end well for the occupants of the home. The "take what you want, but just don't hurt us" plea does not usually work. The invaders did not just force their way into your home to ask for permission to take your belongings and then to leave quietly. They will of course take whatever they want, but unfortunately if given the opportunity they will also hurt you. It stands to reason that if theft was the only motive, the invaders would choose a time when the home was unoccupied.

The typical home invaders are well aware that you and your family are home, and they generally plan it that way. Home invasions are usually very violent, and the invaders typically come well armed, and prepared with rope, duct tape, handcuffs, tie wraps and other means of restraining and controlling their victims.

During a WCS, the risk of violent crimes, including home invasions, can increase dramatically, and law enforcement may not be available to respond as quickly as they normally would. Keeping your family safe from criminals will require more than just dialing 911 or owning a gun.

Here Are Some Ways to Help You Protect Yourself and Your Family:

- Do a security audit of your home – think in terms of layered security. Make sure that all exterior doors, windows and other possible entry points and in good working order and strong. If there are weaknesses or deficiencies, get those fixed right away.
- Install quality deadbolts, high security locks and reinforced strike plates. There is a huge difference between a quality deadbolt and a cheap imitation. This is an investment in your life.
- Install solid wood or metal doors with pinned, multiple hinges in all bedrooms. This will slow down any intruders.
- Install an alarm system, and make sure to have a panic button in several key locations throughout the house.

(Especially the master bedroom and other rooms where you and your family spend most of your time.)

- Install a security camera system.
- Install plenty of lighting around the perimeter of your home.
- Keep the landscaping low all around your house. Plant thorny bushes around all windows. Overgrown yard plants give criminals a good place to hide in ambush mode.
- Have either impact proof windows, or install a security safety film on the inside of the windows to hold the pieces of glass together if the glass is broken. This creates a strong barrier and will buy you some extra time.
- Develop a sound home security and self-defense plan.
- Have open discussions with all members of the household and make sure they all understand the plan, and what they must do in the event of a home invasion.
- Conduct regular safety drills with your family, and explain what they should, and should not do in the event of a home invasion.
- Establish an emergency code word that will alert all family members of a possible invasion.
- Never open the door for someone you don't know – especially at night. Teach young children to never open the door for anyone and to immediately call an adult.
- Have a basic Safe/Panic Room to provide a secured location for all family members to shelter in place. This will buy you time, see below.
- If you own a weapon, make sure that you know how to use it and that you are prepared to do so.
- Get appropriate training for yourself and all adult family members who will use or have access to a firearm.
- Never, ever leave spare keys hidden outside the hose. If a family member loses his or her home key immediately change or re-key all the locks.

- When you arrive home always look around the perimeter of your house or apartment for signs of a break in or any suspicious activity. If you see any broken/forced doors or windows, don't enter the property. Just keep going and call the police from a safe distance.
- Don't volunteer to be a victim.

A home invasion can happen at any time and to anybody. You should always be vigilant and alert. Don't allow yourself to slip into that comfortable complacency, assuming that nothing will happen. Properly secure your home, and employ common sense security and safety measures all the time, not just during a WCS. But before, during and after any crisis, be especially alert and push your security awareness to the next level.

The Safe Room

The first priority in any crisis is security and personal safety. You should prepare your home to make it as difficult as possible for any intruder to gain access. Strong physical barriers, and warning systems will go a long way to protecting your family. For an additional layer of security you should consider investing in a basic safe/panic room. Anything you can do to make it more difficult for them to get in, or to delay their entry, will buy you valuable time to flee, to call for help, or to arm yourself. Once the intruders are inside, you have very few options. A safe room gives you a secure physical structure between you and your attackers, and buys you more time. A secure safe room will also offer additional protection during a storm, and other weather related events.

Here are some ideas to help you prepare a safe room:
- Study the layout of your home and decide which room, closet, or bathroom is situated in the best location for your purposes. You should try to find a location bordered by as many solid (exterior) walls as possible. Sheetrock offers

little protection against a determined intruder. A closet, or some other small room, can be fortified by installing layers of thick plywood under the sheetrock walls.

- If possible have several rooms prepared in advance since, if you have a large home, you may find yourself on the other side of the house from your safe room when a threat occurs. Having more than one location increases the odds in your favor.

- The room should have the least number of windows possible. If there are windows make sure that they have impact glass or security film especially if the room is on the ground level.

- Install solid core wood or metal doors. Make sure to use three, preferably four, pinned hinges and a reinforced strike plate and deadbolt. If your door can be easily kicked in by an intruder, it's worthless for a safe room.

- Make sure that your safe room allows you access to
  o   An Alarm Key pad and/or panic button.
  o   A charged cell phone and a land line.
  o   Cover to protect against incoming gun fire.
  o   Your self-defense firearms, ammunition and a flashlight.

- Additionally your safe room should contain the following supplies:
  o   First Aid and Trauma kit for addressing emergency injuries and bleeds. Also include some N95 Masks.
  o   Small supply of drinking water and food – may seem ridiculous but you don't know how long it will be before you can come out safely. Better safe than sorry; nothing crazy just a few meals ready to eat (MREs), some protein bars, and a few bottles of waters. It's important to remember that you may use the safe room for reasons other than a home invasion, such as a serious storm, or other severe weather.

o   Fire extinguishers – Hopefully not something you will ever have to deal with, but you never know.

o   Ballistic vests or body armor. May seem a bit extreme until the intruders start shooting up your house. If you can afford it, get it.

o   A flashlight with a red colored lens to save your night vision and to allow you to see what you are doing without having to put out a lot of light.

o   If you have security cameras on your property, a monitor in your safe room will allow you to see what is happening outside. Cameras, alarms, phone lines can all be disabled by criminals, but they are still worth having since not all home invaders will be that sophisticated, and you should use every advantage you have.

Security/Self-Defense Limitations:

No matter how fit, healthy, strong, well prepared and well armed you may be – you can only do so much. Every situation is unique, and a serious, objective assessment should always be done well in advance of any threat. During any crisis the physical threats may become overwhelming. It's important to remember that the goal is never to fight, but to get yourself and your family away from the danger and to live. Fighting should always be the last resort. Here are some important issues to consider before you engage in any sort of physical or armed confrontation:

•   Is this a fight you can ultimately win? And is it really worth the risks?

•   Is there a way to possibly defuse the situation and to avoid violence?

•   Do you have enough people to do the job properly? Setting up a self-defense plan may require having enough trained people to stand guard 24 hours a day.

•   No matter how tough you may be, you can't do it all yourself; you need to sleep, eat, etc. During all these activities you leave yourself vulnerable to attack if you are trying to carry the load all by yourself.

- Do you have a defensible position?
- Do you really want to risk an actual firefight and are you prepared for the possible consequences?

Don't ever make the mistake of underestimating an attacker. Perform an honest evaluation of your strengths and weaknesses and plan accordingly. And whenever possible avoid any confrontations, armed or otherwise.

7: All the Bugs–Getting Out, Staying Put & Getting Home

"Should I Stay or Should I Go"
-The Clash

In This Chapter:
Essentially the *Bugs* can be divided into three major categories:
1. **Bugging-Out** (Getting out fast to a safer location)
2. **Bugging-In** (Staying put/staying safe in your home or some other secure structure/location and keeping a very low profile.
3. **Bugging-Back** (Getting back home after some unforeseen threat and/or disaster that occurs while you are away from your home)

Why the *Bugs* Matter

Imagine that you and your family are awakened in the middle of the night by a powerful earthquake. Your house is badly damaged and you only have minutes to get out. You and your family are unhurt, but your neighborhood has been devastated and many of your neighbors are seriously injured or trapped in the rubble. You have literally left your home barefoot and with only the clothes on your back – more than likely pajamas or underwear. Several strong aftershocks and the resulting structural damage to your home make it completely unsafe to enter under any circumstances. From what you can see the streets are mostly closed or otherwise impassable, and in any case your vehicle was also badly damaged in the quake and is largely buried under several layers of rubble.

Until help arrives, you are on your own. What will you do? The streets are covered with debris and downed power lines. In the distance, you can see large fires and expanding plumes of smoke blanketing the horizon. All around you are the sounds of panic and despair; from blaring sirens to the moans and cries of the injured. There is death, destruction and misery everywhere you look. First responders are overwhelmed, and it will probably be some time before they get to you and your neighbors. Deep in your heart, you know that true help might not arrive for days, possibly even much longer. You must do what you can to help your neighbors and then get your family to safety. Exposed and in the open they have no chance of survival. You have some relatives in another part of town who may be able to help, but the only way to get there is to walk. Under these conditions, what would normally be a 30 minute drive could take several days on foot. Public transportation is out of the question. You have no idea of the conditions you will encounter within your immediate neighborhood; much less what awaits you further down the road. Everything you ever owned is buried in the ruins of what used to be your home - clothes, shoes, identification, your wallet, money, food, water, prescription medicines, insurance and financial papers, contact information for friends and relatives, even your cell phone was lost. You need to get yourself and your family to a safer location, but are you properly prepared and equipped to undertake such a journey? You need food, water, protection from the elements and from other far more dangerous situations that you might encounter on the road. If only you had planned ahead.

For the family in this scenario, the circumstances seem pretty desperate. These types of disasters happen more often than you might think – and that's the scariest part of all. With a little planning and some advance preparations this family would have been in a very different situation. No amount of planning will ever prevent disasters such as these from occurring. But, if this family had prepared a bug-out bag with some of the basic essentials, food, water, extra clothing, shoes, a flashlight and access to copies of important documents and contact information, their circumstances could have been substantially better.

Bugging-Out - Getting Out Fast to a Safer Location

Bugging-Out is a survival term that commonly refers to leaving your present location, in a very big hurry, usually under emergency circumstances and evacuating to a safer, more secure, destination. In essence, it is the opposite of bugging-in. When a crisis strikes, there are two options – bugging-in (staying) or bugging-out (leaving). Both situations can be complicated, but bugging-out is usually far more hazardous, and requires much more advance planning.

Bugging-out is extremely dangerous and should only be undertaken as a last resort, and if there are no other options available. Absent extraordinary circumstances, your home will usually be the safest place to be during and after a major crisis. If you have planned well, your home will afford you food, water, relative security and the *home court* advantage. Taking off, loaded-down with gear, with no place to go can be very scary and will expose you and your family to whatever dangers lurk on the streets/roads and other open spaces. Outside your doors there may be many dangerous situations, including, but not limited to, riots, looters, bandits or just some very hungry and thirsty people willing to do just about anything to get their hands on your supplies. These desperate people may stop at nothing to take whatever you have that they want. Worse yet, some of them may even take your life after taking everything else, just because they can. Remember that after a WCS, law and order may be nothing more than a distant memory, and most criminals never pass up a target of opportunity.

Once you leave the relative safety of your home, there is no telling what you will find, or how far you will have to travel to reach a point of safety. The lack of gasoline, food, water and appropriate security are all issues you will need to consider before bugging-out. On the other hand, if your home is destroyed or rendered uninhabitable, and there are no options in the immediate vicinity, then you may have no choice. In that case, hopefully, you will have planned ahead and secured a viable retreat location that is secure, and well stocked with supplies. Hopefully, you will also have a realistic plan to get to your destination in one piece. If not, you should start planning as soon as possible.

The Realities of Bugging-Out

I often hear people talk about their Bug-Out plan and how if things get really bad they will grab their Bug-out Bag (BOB) and disappear into the wilderness, presumably to live off the land. I always think to myself – good luck. Most of the people who say these things have no idea of the challenges they will face, or what skills they will need to survive such challenges. While the romantic notion of just taking off with your BOB and guns, and roughing it in the woods may work in the movies, in real life it is a literal death sentence. In the wilderness there are a dozen of things that can easily kill an unprepared, untrained and insufficient conditioned person. Absent some very hardcore survival training the majority of us average folks will not last more than a few days in the wilderness. And, in any event, there are not many true wilderness locations within walking distance from the majority of most urban centers. To reach a true wilderness area that will offer you the possibility of shelter, food, water and distance from the hoards, you will have to travel long and hard from most cities. The trip alone may kill you, or you will most likely run out of food and water long before you ever get to your destination. Remember water alone adds approximately eight pounds to your pack for every gallon you carry. Add to that your food, guns, ammunition, and other supplies, and your load can get really heavy, really fast; figure sixty to eighty pounds on your back. Traveling by foot, under these circumstances is not something most people can do without substantial training and physical conditioning. I don't say these things to discourage you; but before you risk your life, make sure that you, and your group, are prepared physically and mentally for the challenges that you will face.

Bugging-out has its purpose, but so does bugging-in. Make sure you know and understand the difference; making the wrong decision, at that crucial moment, could cost you your life.

At minimum, your plan should address the following issues:

- **Bug-Out location** – Do you have a specific location. Is it within driving distance using one tank of gas? If not, how much gas will you need and where will you be able to get that gas during a crisis? Can your vehicle carry extra gas? Do you have the option of safely and securely storing extra gas along the route? Would there be friendly places on-route to get rest, shelter, security, and to pick up supplies? If driving is not an option, is your retreat within a reasonable distance if you need to walk or ride a bicycle?

- **Bug-Out Vehicle** – How appropriate is your bug-out Vehicle? Will it carry everything you need to bring to survive the journey? How reliable is it mechanically? Will it safely and securely go off-road if the planned roads are blocked or otherwise unusable? Will it afford you the necessary level of security if you are attacked?

- **Supplies** – How much food, water, medical supplies, guns and ammunition can your bug-out vehicle carry? Are your supplies packed to allow you to quickly load them into your vehicle? Do you have supplies at your intended destination? Are there friendly places along the route that would allow you the option of securely storing extra food, water and other supplies?

- **Travel Route** – Do you have a pre-calculated route to your retreat location? Do you have alternate routes in the event that the chosen roads are blocked, destroyed or too dangerous? Do you have paper maps of all highways, roads, and local streets? If your vehicle runs out of gas, breaks down or is otherwise disabled, can you finish the journey on foot? And would you want to?

If your bug-out Plan doesn't address all these issues then you have some serious planning to do. This is not an area where you can merely take off and hope for the best, especially if you will be traveling with your family. If you are serious about having a viable plan, you need to do your research and have answers to the above questions way in advance of any crisis.

NOTE: Make it a point to always have a full tank of gas in your vehicle. The moment you see the gauge approaching three quarters of a tank, fill it up. No need to wait for a crisis to discover that the only thing holding you back from leaving quickly is a near empty gas tank. Once the crisis hits, you can expect long gas lines or worse yet, closed stations.

The Streets and Roads

Here in Miami, we are within twenty-five miles of the Turkey Point Nuclear Generating Station. A little further north there are two additional nuclear reactors located a mere 130 miles from Miami. South Florida is located straight in the path of what is commonly referred to as "Hurricane Alley". I have often thought about how people in Miami and surrounding communities, would react to the news of a containment failure at any of these facilities, or to the news of a major storm requiring an all-out evacuation of South Florida. There would be mass panic, horror, pandemonium, and as always, denial. But most of all, there would be a northward vehicle stampede of epic proportions. With so many people (over five million) all trying to get out at the same time, the roads north would very quickly become giant parking lots. Trapped in total gridlock, these vehicles would eventually run out of gas and be abandoned, essentially blocking the roads, leaving their passengers stranded in the middle of nowhere, with no food, no water, and at the mercy of whatever crisis they were trying to escape. Out in the open most people would quickly succumb to heatstroke, dehydration or the ever present criminal element that always seem to show up at the worst possible time. If there was ever a situation requiring an immediate bug-out, a nuclear containment failure would surely top the list. But, if this nightmare WCS ever actually happened, few people in Miami would survive. However, if there is any chance of getting out, *the early bird would probably get the worm.* Meaning, if the moment you heard the news, you grabbed your family and your BOB and headed out, your chances would be substantially better. In a situation such as this, you would need to grab your bag and leave within minutes. While most people wasted time packing luggage, running to the ATM, loading up the car with junk and trying to fill up at the gas station, you could be well ahead of the crowd. To act that quickly you would need to be very well prepared - enter the BOB.

The Bug-Out Bag (BOB)

An effective BOB really can't be bought, it has to be made by its owner, and carefully tailored to the intended purpose. What I mean by this is that the contents of any good BOB must be customized to the individual needs of the owner, the environment, and the time of year in which it will be used. What works for someone in South Florida, might seem ridiculous to someone living in Nebraska. Similarly, a bag equipped for the winter in the cold northern states will be vastly different than one set-up for use during summer.

A good BOB must contain items that you are familiar with, and know how to use. If you put-together the bag yourself you will know what's in it, why it's there and how to use it. Buying an off-the-shelf BOB or 72 hour kit may be easier, less time consuming, and may even seem less expensive – until you really need it. During a crisis is not time to discover that all you really have is a fancy bag filled with mostly useless, impractical stuff that you are not familiar with and can't use. Make your own, you won't regret it.

A good BOB should contain what you need and nothing more. Choosing what to include and what to leave out is probably the most difficult decision you will make when putting together your bag. Given a choice, most of us would take everything we could carry, unfortunately weight, and space limitations will determine how much you can realistically carry. One thing is to throw a bag into a vehicle, it's quite another to have to carry it yourself. Most people tend to underestimate just how difficult it is to carry so much weight over long distances using nothing but their own two feet. If you have any doubts give it a test run one weekend and see how it goes. My guess is that after a few miles you will have a very different notion of what is, and what is not, going in your bag.

For the bag itself get a sturdy book bag with heavy duty padded straps – black is a great color. Try to avoid the *military/tactical* looking bags since these will draw unwelcomed attention to you, and possibly invite trouble. The contents list below is tailored to the conditions commonly found in South Florida and other hot and humid environments, but the list also contains many items that will be relevant in any environment. For us in South Florida, summer seems to last all year long. We get a few semi-cold days, but nothing crazy. I would never pack a heavy coat, winter gloves, or any other cold weather type stuff in my BOB. But in colder climates, those items are a necessity.

Here is a sample list of some basic items to help you get started, make sure to adapt your contents to your individual needs, your environment and the time of year. Remember the contents of this bag may one day help save your life.

1. Compass & Map of Local Area (Clearly mark locations of police, fire stations, hospitals, natural water sources, and other places of interest. Do this well in advance of any WCS. Learn how to use a compass and make sure to have one in your pack.

2. Light Weight Energy Food, Protein Bars, MREs, Snacks, Hard Candy, Gum

3. Bottled Water, Portable Water Filter, Water Purification Tablets or iodine.

4. First Aid Kit – Small Kit with a little of everything you may need.

5. Moleskin – Helps protect sensitive parts of your feet if you are walking long distances

6. Sun Screen & Bug Repellent.
7. Multitool, Large & Small Knife.
8. Fire Starter, Waterproof Matches, Lighter(s).
9. Soap, Small Hand Towels, Antibacterial Gel.
10. Plastic Tarp, Rain Poncho, Bungee Cord(s)
11. Extra Clothes, Hat, Lightweight Gloves and walking shoes.
12. Cash (Small Bills & Coins) – No less than $250.00.
13. Sterno (1 Can), Light Sticks (2-6), Matches or Lighter.
14. LED Flashlight (Hand Crank Preferred) or with Extra Batteries.
15. Radio (Hand Crank Preferred) or with Extra Batteries.
16. Roll(s) of Duct and Electrical Tape.
17. 550 Black Para Cord (100 Feet Minimum).
18. Prescription Medication(s), Toothbrush, dental floss.
19. Masks, (N95 minimum), Nitrile Gloves.
20. Potassium Iodide Tablets (Iosat, Thyrosafe or Thyroshield).
21. Firearms and Extra Magazines and Ammunition, Pepper Spray, Baton, etc.
22. Copies of Important Documents in case you lose your wallet/purse, (Passport, Drivers License, Social Security Card, and Concealed Weapons Permit).
23. Memory Stick containing copies of important papers, scanned copies of legal documents, etc.
24. List of Important Contact Information, phone numbers, addresses, etc.
25. Pre-Paid Calling Card. Pay phones are an uncommon sight nowadays; but there are still some out there. After a disaster cell service may be compromised or your phone may be lost or damaged, some landlines may still be working. Having a pre-paid calling card may come in very handy.
26. Small stuffed Animal or Small Toy for Kids – Will Help Keep Them Quiet and Relaxed.

In colder climates make sure to add weather appropriate clothing and accessories, gloves, hats, boots, hand warmers, insulated sleeping bag, etc.

Keep it Current

Start out with a basic BOB, but go through it at least once every three months and keep it up to date and relevant. Take out all the contents, inspect their condition and repack. As conditions change remove and replace items of limited value. Always pack your bag in the order in which you expect you might need the contents. For obvious reasons you would never bury your extra ammunition magazines down at the very bottom of the BOB. Also if you are forced to walk out of your location, you don't want to be emptying the entire contents of your BOB, for all to see, searching for an item way down at the bottom. The contents you except to need first should be at the very top, and don't store your entire stash, of anything, in one location. For example keep you money in several different pockets. If you must take out cash to pay for something you don't want to pull out a large amount of cash in front of strangers.

Finally, keep your BOB in a secure location, away from prying eyes and children, but handy enough that you would be able to grab it and go without delays or complications. Don't ever raid you BOB for anything you don't intend to replace immediately. Adjust your supplies as the seasons change, and make sure to periodically rotate your contents and freshen up your food supplies, water, batteries, etc.

Bugging-In (Sheltering-In-Place

Bugging-In is the opposite of Bugging-Out. Bugging-In is basically staying put in your home or some other secure location and keeping a very low profile. But staying in your own home will require you to rely only on the preparations you have made. For reasons previously discussed, this will usually be your first choice, circumstances permitting. However, in order to Bug-In you must have the necessary supplies: food, water and of course adequate resources to establish and maintain an acceptable level of security.

In most Bugging-In situations you can figure that you will probably not have access to grocery stores, supermarkets, gas stations or any electricity, water or other utilities. You can also assume that there will be plenty of people who did not prepare and some may be trying to take what you have; thus the part about security. There are many advantages to Bugging-In and many disadvantages. In most instances the circumstances will dictate your course of action. But try to be proactive and don't just react to circumstances.

Bugging-Back (Getting Back Home)

In most urban areas millions of people drive or commute using public transportation into crowded downtown areas filled with high-rise buildings, heavily congested roads, and limited options for entering or existing the city center. If you are one of those people, you will have some special challenges that you must plan for. If there is a crisis and it catches you at work, how are you going to get out of where you are, and get home safely? Will you be prepared or will you be one of the many people wandering around in shock, waiting for help that often doesn't come for many hours, or possible days?

This is especially important if you

- Commute in a large city; ride a train or take public transportation.
- Work in a large office building with many floors.
- Commute in or around an area prone to heavy traffic, and congestion.

Even if you have a Bug-out-Bag it is useless to you at this point – it's probably home. Even if you could get to your B.O.B., how much good would it do you in this situation? A Get Home Bag (GHB) *contains* an entirely different set of tools, and serves an entirely different purpose - to help you get back home from wherever you happen to be when a crisis hits. If you don't have a GHB in your office or place of business, you should. On 9/11 many of the World Trade Center survivors were forced to walk home over long distances. Many of these folks were wearing heels or dress shoes and standard business attire.

Get Home Bag (GHB)

Your GBH should contain items/supplies to help you:

- Make it through the aftermath of a crisis or disaster.
- Signal for help, or get out of a building such as Flashlights, or light sticks.
- On what could be a very long walk home; with items such as High Energy Food, Water and Comfortable Shoes.
- Clearly a GHB is not a BOB. There is some obvious overlap, but a GBH is usually much smaller, lighter in weight, with more specific tools, and with one purpose – to help get you home.

Here Are Some Suggested Items for a Basic Get Home Bag (GHB)

1. Compact First Aid Kit – Stop Bleeding and Cover Wounds
2. Small LED Flashlight, Extra Batteries, Light Stick. Crank light is even better.
3. Small Knife, and a Multi-tool
4. Compass & Map of Local Area (Clearly mark locations of police & fire stations, hospitals, natural water sources, and other places of interest. Do this well in advance of any WCS, and make sure that you can read a map and use a compass.
5. Sun Screen & Bug Repellent – Climate and Season Driven.
6. Eye Protection – Clear Impact-Proof Glasses to Protect Your Eyes from dust, debris or other foreign matter; it would be very difficult to get home if you can't see.
7. Ear Protection – To help reduce the sound of Sirens and other ear-damaging Noises.
8. Bottled Water, Energy & Power Bars – For Hydration and Energy

9. Antibacterial Gel, Pre-moistened Towels – To Disinfect Hands.
10. Rain Poncho, Extra Clothes – To Stay Dry and Comfortable.
11. Comfortable Walking Shoes – You May Have to Walk it Home.
12. Moleskin – Will Help Protect Sensitive Parts of Your Feet Against Blisters.
13. Cash (Small Bills & Some Coin) – ATMs may be inoperable or depleted.
14. N95 Masks, Gloves – Protect Against Dust and Other Contaminants.
15. Small Supply of Prescription Medications – In Case You Can't Get Home Right Away.
16. Extra Pair of Prescription Glasses.
17. Copies of Important Documents (Passport, Driver's License, and Concealed Weapons Permits) in case you lose your wallet/Purse.
18. List of Emergency Contacts & Phone Numbers.
19. Pepper Spray/Handgun with Extra Ammunition (Optional)
20. Pre-Paid Calling Card. After a disaster cell service may be compromised or your phone may be lost or damaged, some landlines may still be working. Having a pre-paid calling card may come in very handy to call for help or let loved know where you are.

Keep your bag at your office, place of business, or workplace. Caution – some employers do not allow firearms on their premises under any circumstances. If this is true in your case, you will need to find alternatives. As with a BOB, keep your GHB current and relevant. Update and rotate supplies often. Test your equipment and make sure it is working properly. Please don't just throw your GHB in a closet and forget about it. Remember, the day you need it, you will need it desperately.

8: Survival Hygiene and Sanitation–Why You Should Come Clean

"Cleanliness becomes more important when godliness is unlikely."

-P. J. O'Rourke

In This Chapter:

- In a survival situation sanitation is about where people go to the bathroom, and what happens to their waste.
- Sanitation is also about creating the proper environment to prevent, or at least, minimize, the spread of contamination and diseases.
- Lack of proper hygiene and sanitation can kill you just as surely as lack of food, water or security.
- Sanitation is probably one of the most neglected areas in survival planning.
- Proper planning and preparations can help you keep yourself clean, healthy and in high spirits.

Hygiene and sanitation are not topics that most people expect to see in a survival plan. I have seen many otherwise elaborate survival plans that totally neglect these issues. When most of us think about urban survival, our focus usually shifts to food, water, first aid, weapons, ammunition, etc., and rightly so. But few of us ever consider or plan on how we will stay clean, or maintain a healthy and sanitary environment in which to live, sleep, cook and eat; and even fewer of us think about how, during a WCS, we will effectively and safely get rid of our waste. The good news is that preparing will not require complicated planning or expensive equipment or gear. But, it will require some basic planning, supplies, and a clear understanding of how to avoid the things that can really hurt you. Ignore this topic and you may one day regret it.

How Things Will Change After a WCS

Normally, a seemingly limitless amount of clean water comes into our homes. To use this water all we need to do is open a faucet. It arrives fresh, clean, sanitized, disinfected and ready to be used anyway we see fit. We routinely make use of this water to drink, cook, wash and yes we also use it to flush our bodily waste down the drain and out to the sewer – few of us ever stop to give this process a second thought, and most of us take it completely for granted. During *normal* times many of us will take a nice, hot shower or a bath on a daily basis. On average during a 5 minute shower, you will consume anywhere between 10-25 gallons of water per shower – depending on the shower head's flow rate. A bath requires even more water, about 25-50 gallons per bath.

During *normal* times many of us routinely wash our hands. According to the Centers for Disease Control and Prevention (CDC), hand washing is the most effective way to prevent illness and the spread of infection. As we all know, there are many bacteria and contaminants that come in contact with our hands on a daily basis just by touching surfaces touched by others; this is especially true in highly populated urban centers. If after exposure, you don't wash your hands before eating or preparing food, you could ingest these bacteria, making you extremely sick. Some of the most common and problematic bacteria and virus are:

- **E. Coli Poisoning**
- **Cold and Flu Virus**
- **Fecal Bacteria**
- **Salmonella**
- **Norovirus**
- **MRSA Bacteria**

Any of these will cause you to have a very bad day - nausea, vomiting, diarrhea and sometimes dehydration. During a WCS, if left untreated, any of these conditions can easily kill you.

During *normal* times:
- We rarely have a need to question the quality of the water we consume.
- We *do our business,* and press a handle that flushes all the nastiness down the drain.
- We routinely have access to clean running water and soap to wash our hands and bodies.
- We bag our solid waste and place it out on the curb where it's picked up and disposed of, far from sight. Most people have no idea where their waste ends up, and even fewer care. We're just happy to see that the garbage can is empty when we arrive home at the end of the day.

By now, it should be evident where we're going with all this. After a WCS:
- Water may be contaminated, or otherwise unusable for our everyday needs.
- Water may be in very short supply and strictly reserved for drinking and possibly some cooking.
- Garbage/solid waste collection may be delayed, suspended or cancelled altogether.
- Sewer pump stations may be inoperable, damaged, or temporarily disabled – this will cause your drain pipes to either not work or to start backing-up.

The end result may be that you will have to deal with, and resolve, a daily waste problem that if mismanaged, or worse yet ignored, can very quickly become your very own personal nightmare. Dealing with this new reality will be a huge challenge for the prepared; for the unprepared, it will be completely unmanageable. The next time you flip the switch in your kitchen, and the light comes on, remember that with relatively inexpensive and easily accessible power, everything has become better, easier, faster and more efficient. As a result, just about everything in our life is electrical. Even toilets have started losing their flush handles in favor of an electrical sensor that automatically flushes. (We can now add toilets and urinals to the long list of things that won't work if the electricity goes off). The sewer systems in all major cities use electrical pumping stations to keep the waste flowing in the right direction. The day the power fails the sewers will very quickly stop flowing.

Sanitation and Disease

Human waste (feces) is full of dangerous bacteria that can cause many nasty diseases – cholera, infectious hepatitis, typhoid, etc. Lack of proper sanitation can bring the feces into contact with hands, water, food and other things that can potentially transfer the bacteria back to us, and make us very sick. Once the contamination begins so will the nightmare.

In most developed countries clean drinking water and proper waste disposal has all but eliminated the majority of these problems, but it has not always been so. A little more than 100 years ago many large American cities, New York City for example, were centers of disease and infection. Child death rates back then were almost as high as they are today in third-world countries.

In modern times, water safety is still seriously compromised for millions of people around the world because of poor sanitation and lack of hygiene. The majority of illness, in the developing world, is caused by lack of sanitation and infection with fecal matter.

Here in the U.S., in the aftermath of any WCS, we can very quickly lose all the advantages that we enjoy, but rarely appreciate – clean, safe water, flushing toilets, the sewer system and solid waste pick-up and disposal. The lack of sanitation and proper waste disposal following a major disaster will quickly create an environment that can, directly or indirectly, cause serious infections and life threatening conditions for millions, especially in the large urban centers.

What You Need to Know:

In the face of a wide-scale urban disaster, your best option may be to get out of the immediate area, and into a remote, less densely populated region. But for many reasons, this may not always be a viable option. You may not have a safe place to go, or even if you do, you may not have a safe way to get there. If getting out is not an option, you may have little choice but to stay put and wait it out.

Over the long-run, urban areas can potentially become death traps in the aftermath of a major disaster, but in the short-term there is much that you can do to make it safer, and certainly more tolerable. However, this will require having a plan and having the necessary supplies. The following guidelines detail some of the basic planning and preparations you should consider.

Water Disinfection:

This book devotes an entire chapter to water and water disinfection (See chapter 3). We will not repeat all that information here. Suffice it to say that you should always disinfect any suspect water, and all water is suspect until confirmed otherwise. This includes water that you intend to use for washing, cooking or for any other purpose that might in some way bring the disinfected water in contact with people.

Hand Washing:

If your water supply is somehow compromised, washing your hands with contaminated water will only help to spread the contamination even faster. You will need a way to keep your hands clean while using very limited amounts of disinfected water. Remember you'll want to save as much of the safe water as possible for drinking and cooking. Even without running water, there are a number of methods that can help you keep your hands clean, here are a few:

- Use an alcohol gel or some other form of antimicrobial hand sanitizer; these products can be quite effective in the short term but will eventually run out.
- Wash your hands using a small amount of water and soap in a basin or sink, rinse in another receptacle using again a small amount of clean water, dry off with a paper towel, that you will throw away. Try not to handle your water containers with infected hands. If necessary, have someone else in your group pour the clean water for you to use.
- Prepare a solution of three parts clean water, and one part chlorine bleach and put it in a spray bottle. Have another person spray your hands while you rub them together. Rinse and air dry or use a clean paper towel.

Stop the Spread of Disease and Infection

In any survival situation, preventing a problem is always better that struggling to fix it after the fact. Many water-related diseases that have all but disappeared from our modern day society can very quickly reemerge after a major disaster, when basic hygiene and sanitation are compromised. To stop the spread you'll need to take some basic precautions, especially when treating infected individuals. Most of these diseases are spread if:

- You eat food or drink beverages that have been handled by a person who is ill, or is a carrier.
- If you ingest water contaminated by the feces of an ill person, or a carrier.

Many of these diseases are quite common in third world, or developing countries, where hand washing is not as common and water is likely to be contaminated with sewage.

Here are some basic precautions to help prevent the spread:

- Drink canned or bottled water whenever possible.
- Boil, or treat suspect water with a chorine product or household bleach. (See Chapter 3)

- Use disinfected water to wash, and prepare food.
- Use disinfected water to wash any items that you will use in eating or preparing food. Better yet use disposables.
- Wash your hands with soap and disinfected water as often as possible, but especially after using the toilet, before preparing food, or after taking care of someone who has diarrhea or that is known, or suspected, to be ill.
- Use plastic and/or paper disposable plates and disposable plastic utensils, and throw out all used plates and utensils so that no one can come in contact with the potentially infected items.
- Always store the clearly marked disinfected water in a clean, covered, container to prevent recontamination.
- Use protective clothing, gloves and a surgical mask when treating someone who has diarrhea, or that is known, or suspected, to be ill. (The mask is primarily intended to stop you from inadvertently touching your mouth or face with dirty hands.)
- Use protective clothing, gloves and a surgical mask when disposing of feces or cleaning out your toilet facilities or latrine.
- Use plastic bags to hold feces/diapers, and dispose of all such plastic bags in plastic or metal garbage cans as far away from your food, water and living area.

Baking Soda – A Miracle Product

There are literally hundreds of uses for baking soda. During a crisis, baking soda makes a perfect substitute for many household products. It's versatile, inexpensive, free of toxic chemicals, effective and it stores very well. Without getting into the science, just know that baking soda regulates pH, and it works. Besides its obvious uses such as making homemade cookies and making the refrigerator smell better, there are many practical uses for baking soda; especially during a crisis when personal care, cleaning, and deodorizing products, may be in short supply. The following is a short list of some of the uses:

- Make Toothpaste – Make a paste from baking soda and hydrogen peroxide to brush your teeth.
- Mouthwash – Use one teaspoon in half a glass of water, swish, spit, and rinse to keep mouth fresh and odor free.
- Clean Dentures - 2 teaspoons of baking soda dissolved in a small bowl of water will keep dentures and oral pieces clean, and odor free.
- Antacid – A safe and effective antacid to relieve heartburn, sour stomach and acid indigestion.
- Deodorant – Apply baking soda to underarms to reduce odor.
- Foot Soak – Dissolve 4 tablespoons of baking soda in warm water to soak and refresh tired feet.
- Insect Bites & Itchy Skin – Make a paste from baking soda and water, and apply to affected area.
- Hand Cleaner – Scrub away dirt with a paste of 3 parts baking soda to 1 part water, rinse and dry.
- Clean pots, pans, dishes and kitchen utensils – Add baking soda to dish water to help cut grease.
- Cleaning Solution – Mix baking soda with water to make a simple, but effective cleaning solution for the home.
- Deodorizer – Use baking soda to help absorb foul odors, just about anywhere.
- Deodorize Shoes, Boots and Sneakers – Put some baking soda inside shoes to control odor.
- Deodorize Garbage Cans – Sprinkle in garbage receptacles to control odors.
- Fire Extinguisher – Baking soda helps extinguish grease or electrical fires. Throw baking soda at the base of a flame to put out the fire.

What You Will Need

Here is a sample list of some basic items to help you get started, make sure to adapt your purchases to your individual needs, your environment and the time of year. Remember the use of these items may one day help save your life.

1. Five (5) Gallon Buckets – These buckets have many uses and are extremely durable. Have as many of these as you can afford.
2. Chlorine Bleach (Unscented)
3. Spray Bottles – Various Sizes
4. Anti-Bacterial Soap – Liquid and Bars
5. Anti-Bacterial Gels and Hand Sanitizers
6. Anti-Bacterial Wipes
7. Disinfecting Sprays – For Odor Control and Surface Disinfection
8. Alcohol Wipes – For Sanitation and Disinfection
9. Heavy Duty Plastic Garbage Bags – Various Sizes
10. Portable/Chemical Toilets
11. Face Masks
12. Nitrile Gloves – Large Assortment of Different Sizes
13. Eye Shield/Protection – To Protect Against Splatter
14. Toilet Paper – Store as Much as Possible
15. Paper Towels - Store as Much as Possible
16. Disposable Plastic or Paper Plates and Cups
17. Disposable Plastic Forks, Spoons, Knives and Serving Utensils
18. Baking Soda – Lots of it.
19. White Vinegar - Lots of it.

Now is the time stock-up on all the necessary supplies. Fortunately, most of these items are relatively inexpensive and non-perishable; if properly stored your supplies will keep for many years.

Nothing you can do will ever be 100% effective in preventing the spread of diseases or contamination. But, there are many precautions that will effectively prevent the majority of these conditions from spreading among the members of your group or family. Make sure to establish and clearly communicate these life saving procedures to all the members of your group

9: Survival Conditioning–Physical & Mental Fortitude

"That which does not kill me makes me stronger."
-Friedrich Nietzsche

In This Chapter:
- A WCS, or any survival scenario, will test your physical capacity and endurance.
- People who are not used to the physical strain and stress of long hours of walking, running and carrying heavy loads will be ill equipped to meet the demands of surviving after a crisis.
- The ability to take physical action at a moment's notice requires a certain level of cardiovascular fitness, and strength, that most people just don't have.
- Crisis or not, your life will dramatically improve if you maintain a healthy lifestyle and a strong, flexible body.
- Eat well, exercise and focus on overall strength and fitness.
- Changing your bad habits should not cost you one penny.
- Building strength, endurance and stamina is possible at any age.
- Get the proper amount of restful sleep, and stop worrying so much.
- Having regular medical and dental check-ups and managing your overall health will ensure that you are in the best possible condition in the event of a WCS.
- Staying current on all relevant vaccinations will ensure that you are protected from common, but avoidable, conditions and diseases.

- Your mind should guide your actions and control your body, not the other way around.

With all the emphasis on survival equipment, supplies and gear, it's easy to forget that in some survival situations the most important factor may well be your personal fitness, health and mental fortitude. Whether it's your ability to endure the physical demands of the circumstances, to walk long distances, or to fend off an attacker; you'll need to be in good physical shape, and to have your mind in the game.

Survival Conditioning

To survive means to stay alive, to overcome some life-threatening situation by whatever means necessary. The most difficult factor in a survival situation is the lack of predictability. One moment you may be minding your own business going about living your life, and without any warning, you may find yourself knee deep in a survival scenario. There may be loud noises, people screaming, wrecked vehicles, injuries and maybe explosions. It may be an earthquake, a fire, an accident, a terrorist attack, or maybe a home invasion. You just never know what might be thrown your way. In some situations, you may need to run very fast to get away from some immediate threat. At other times, you may need to carry a very heavy weight, maybe a pack, or maybe even another person. You may also need to fight off an attacker. You may need to do all these things quickly, effectively and without any assistance. And finally, while you're doing all these amazing feats, you also want to be resistant to injury; since in a survival situation, even a minor injury can put you at grave risk. The better conditioned your body is, the more effective it will be when called into action.

The Physical

We live in a society where physical strength and endurance are not high priorities for many people. Many folks, especially in urban areas, work in jobs that are not physically demanding. The average office worker sits most of the day, in front of a computer monitor with a mouse and a phone. Very few Americans still plow fields or dig ditches; and those who do, use fully mechanized power equipment specifically designed to do most of the work. Many jobs that were once physically demanding are now done by machines that the operator controls from a computer terminal, with a few key strokes, or the aid of a mouse.

But, all of the crisis situations we described above would require instant explosive action and physical stamina, endurance and strength. No matter how many preparations you make, there will always be the possibility that you'll encounter circumstances that will test your physical abilities to the maximum extent possible.

Once the electricity is out, even just doing simple household chores will seem like an extraordinary physical burden for many people who are seriously out of shape. Imagine washing your clothes by hand, scrubbing floors, cleaning and cooking without the help of all those electric household gadgets, that we have all come to love. You will need to use muscles you didn't even know you had. Now imagine having to clear the walkway to your front door after a major storm knocks down trees and scatters debris all over your yard. Imagine cutting, moving and clearing all the debris by hand, using nothing more than simple hand tools and muscle power. To many people this is simply unthinkable. Consider walking many miles carrying your bug-out-bag to a remote location, if your primary residence is destroyed or becomes uninhabitable. Or more importantly, imagine that you are forced to fight off an attacker; or multiple attackers – by hand. Would you be up to the task? Would you have the strength, stamina and endurance to survive such an attack and to prevail? If the answer is "No" now is the time to start readjusting your priorities. Will you spend your weekends sitting in front of that new flat screen TV, hypnotized by that new show that everybody's talking about? Or will you get off the coach and start making an investment in your health, strength and endurance?

There was a time when people worked close to home, many within walking distance. Most people worked long hours in jobs that were purely physical. And even if their jobs weren't entirely physical, most everything they used was powered by "human power" from the type writer, to the adding machine, all required human muscle to function. People routinely walked up many flights of stairs and walked long distances, on a daily basis, without giving it a second thought. Even driving a vehicle required arm and leg strength since both steering and braking systems were fully manual. Most people alive today have grown up with power *everything*. Today everything is electrical.

Ways to Improve Your Level of Survival Fitness and Overall Wellbeing

1. Get checked out - Before starting any exercise program make sure to get a check-up, and discuss any concerns with your doctor. If you can't remember the last time you saw your doctor, or the last time you got a routine physical exam, this is a good time to pick up the phone and make an appointment. If you have any underlying health concerns, getting those addressed should be your first order of business.

2. Establish a baseline and keep a journal to help you remember where you started, and to track your progress.

3. Get motivated – Getting started, and staying with it can be a real challenge, but find what motivates you personally. Most people find it helpful to remember that their efforts are aimed at a very significant goal – having the physical strength to survive.

4. Just get started - It's good to have a plan, but in many situations it may be better to just get out there and start moving. Few of us get much exercise; when we do we're sore for days, sometimes longer. Ease into it, but get started right away. You have probably waited long enough.

5. Push past your limits – You'll be surprised what you can accomplish when you demand more from yourself. Pushing past your limits will also provide you with newfound confidence. Leave your comfort zone and be willing to sweat.

6. Stick with it – lots of people join a gym, start taking classes, begin walking more; then they just stop. Consistency is more important than intensity. Find the activities that you like, and stick with them. Change it up, alternate and add variety, but keep it going.

7. Break the TV habit – folks get home from work, have dinner, and sit in front of the TV, and just never manage to get up until it's time for bed. Sitting in front of the set, will never improve your health, it will diminish it. If you hope to get stronger, faster, and to have more endurance you need to get up and go. TV feeds us mind-garbage, and sitting down is killing you slowly. Where's the upside?

8. Eat right, eat healthy and pass on the unhealthy stuff – Add more nutritious food to your menu. Eat more protein and healthy carbohydrates. Whenever possible eat fresh fruits and vegetables. Keep an open mind and try new foods. If you can afford it, buy organic and avoid processed foods. The food you consume is what fuels your body and mind, and it also provides the building blocks for everything from your bones to the hair on your head. If you feed your body garbage, you can't expect much in return.

9. Stay well hydrated – drink plenty of water and try to avoid sugary beverages.

10. Definitely stay away from or drastically reduce tobacco and alcohol consumption; these things zap you energy and diminish your health.

11. Get your rest – Exercise, good food and proper hydration are all important, but so is good quality rest. Getting a good night's sleep has gotten tougher for many of us. We go to bed with a head full of worries and concerns and we often spend half the night re-playing the day's events in our minds. Get into a routine of winding down an hour or so before bed time. Try to get rid of all the unpleasant thoughts and don't worry about stuff you can't change. And

for goodness sakes don't watch the news before going to bed. If anything, try to read a book, listen to some calming music, or use the opportunity to spend some quiet time with loved ones. Take only happy and positive thoughts to your pillow. Yes, there's a lot of messed up stuff in the world, but you're not going to fix it by worrying about it.

The Survival Mindset, Mind-Over-Matter

When faced with a crisis, some people refuse to give up and they fight literally to their very last breath. On the other side of the spectrum are the people who give up almost immediately - defeated, panicked, scared, and demoralized they lose their will to go on. Once people give up mentally, it's only a matter of time before their bodies follow. No matter how healthy or strong your body may be, your mind must also be strong and resolute. Your willingness to fight on will often determine the outcome of many seemingly hopeless situations.

No one has ever survived a crisis by feeling sorry for themselves and/or by giving up hope. Yet, when faced with the reality of a crisis, some people literally shut-down and become paralyzed with fear, and the inability to make even the smallest decision.

Here are some tips to help you get, and stay focused with the right attitude.

- Proper mindset is the single most important survival factor.
- Positive attitude can save lives. Train your mind to respond under stress, to have the will to prevail no matter the circumstances. Work to instill this attitude in all members of your group.
- Positive Outlook - No matter how bad things get, never quit; know that you will survive. (Never give up and never stop trying).
- Confidence – Don't panic; always look for opportunities. Keep a clear head, and focus on finding solutions, never dwell on the problems.

- Stay Focused - Think positive and think outside the box. (Negative thoughts and actions can bring you down just as quickly as dehydration and exposure).
- Awareness – Develop an awareness of the world around you, and stay focused.
- Assessment – Pay attention, and constantly evaluate risks and opportunities.
- Action – Always be ready to act, and if possible, have a plan.
- Take Charge, Take Responsibility, Organize, and Get it done. Adapt, overcome, and improvise - It's all on you.

Urban survival is as much about preparing physically and mentally, as about security, water, food, and medical supplies. All the stockpiling in the world won't help someone who is mentally and physically unprepared for the challenges associated with a WCS.

10: Preparing for Disaster–The 24 Hour Experiment

In This Chapter:

- Try the 24 hour Experiment - This is where *The Rubber Meets the Road.*
- Most people don't know what they don't know. If there are flaws in your plan or preparations, or worse yet if you haven't made any, this is the best time to identify and assess the weaknesses.
- Step by step survival planning.

Few of us truly know what it is to live, for any extended period of time, without electricity, running water, sewers and public services. But you can get a pretty good idea with a very simple experiment. At the end of this experience, I promise that you will have a much more complete understanding of what an urban survival situation might look, and feel like.

The Experiment

I want to you to pick a day, any day. On that day, you are to get up and go directly to the fuse or breaker box and turn off all the breakers. You will also go to your water main and turn that off. Relax; it's going to be okay. Now, that you have no power and no running water, you will attempt to survive for one entire day (24 solid hours) without electricity or running water. While you're at it, assume that the sewer system is not working, so you can't put anything down the drains since it can't go anywhere and it will just sit in your toilet creating a health hazard. You will only be allowed to use the supplies that you have stocked in your home. Further, you should not rely on any sources outside your own home for food, supplies, water or any assistance.

Here's the scenario. You live in South Florida, the month is August and you have just been hit by a category four hurricane. The storm has passed, but now you and your family have been left without any utilities and the infrastructure in your neighborhood, and surrounding areas, has been badly damaged. The local authorities have urged all residents to stay home since the traffic lights are all down, trees are blocking many streets and the main roads must be kept clear for emergency vehicles and first responders. The power is expected to be out for at least a week, maybe longer. Utility crews are working around-the-clock but they must first focus their efforts on restoring power to hospitals, shelters, police and fire stations, and other vital governmental locations. Additional utility crews are being brought in from unaffected areas, but it will take a while for them to arrive and get started with repairs. Residential neighborhoods are the last item on the utility's *to-do* list. (Here in South Florida it's not unusual to lose power after a major storm; outages have lasted from a few hours to a few weeks. The more extensive the damage to the power lines, transformers, and other vital electrical infrastructure, the longer the repairs will take.

At first, this exercise may not sound like a big deal; in fact it may seem a bit ridiculous, and a big waste of time. But in life there is no substitute for first-hand experience. We may read about some disaster or see it on the news, but few of us take away anything of value from just hearing about someone else's hardships. And although this experiment may seem like an awful waste of a perfectly good day, I promise you one thing – by the end of the 24 hour period you will have an entirely new outlook and appreciation for all the things that you will need to survive an urban style crisis, and for all the things that you should be doing and probably are not. By the way, you can't leave your house, or use any phones, and of course you will try to avoid all contact with the outside world. You may not simply lock up your house and spend the day at the park, and have your meals at a restaurant, or a friend's house – that would defeat the purpose of the exercise.

One last thing, during this experiment you will actually cram one week's worth of activities into one day. Ready? During the next 24 hours you will:

- Figure out a way to prepare meals and eat without any electrical appliances.
- For one meal you will assume that dangerous individuals are roaming your area and you will eat one meal without any sort of cooking or heating to prevent drawing any unnecessary attention to yourself or your location.
- Find, filter and disinfect water for drinking and food preparation. You will use various methods to practice filtering and disinfecting water.
- Set-up an outdoor toilet and shower.
- Do all your business in the makeshift toilet.
- Dispose of all human waste in such a way as to avoid contaminating, your water, your food or your living space.
- Properly collect and dispose of all your garbage to avoid attracting pests, human or otherwise.
- Wash and dry your clothes without the clothes washer & dryer.
- Set-up and implement a self-defense and security plan of action to ensure that a member of your group is always on watch, and ready to alert the other members of any security risk.
- Have a simulated first-aid drill, where one member of your group will act the part of the injured, and the others in your group will administer the appropriate first aid treatment.
- Lastly, at some unexpected point during the day your entire group will need to leave your present location and bug-out to another predetermined location, carrying nothing more than your bug-out bag. You will have no more than three (3) minutes to gather your gear and leave.

If you live in an apartment, condo or multi-unit housing where there is no available outdoor area, or there is a common outside area, your task will be even more difficult. You will need to somehow find a way to perform all these activities within your limitations. You say it can't be done. Well think about it, what would you do if the described scenario actually happened? How would you handle it? And further, assume that the power outage was widespread and that it extended over a large geographic area. In other words, there is no other place to go, except maybe a shelter. Get the picture? You may one day be forced to find a solution to all these problems; why not identify and look for those solutions now before an actual crisis is at your door step? Once the problem is upon you, there may not be any viable solutions available to you. The time to identify and assess the weakness, or strength, of your plan and preparations is before the crisis occurs.

Do I really recommend that you try this experiment? Absolutely! What possible purpose could it serve? Consider some of what you may discover.

1. If you have a plan for Bugging-In and you have made some preparations, this is a great opportunity to test the effectiveness of both the plan, and the preparations. But also to identify weaknesses in your plan. Think of it as a WCS trial run.

2. If you haven't made a plan, or any preparations, this is a great way to find out, first hand, what you should be planning and preparing for, and why.

3. How it really feels to be without any electricity for more than a few minutes, and how you'll function without it.

4. What equipment and tools you may have that are completely worthless without electricity.

5. What tools and equipment you will need to function in the absence of electricity.

6. What your life looks like without modern conveniences.

7. How you will feed yourself without a functioning kitchen, and without buying prepared food, and where that food will come from.

8. How to stay hydrated in the absence of running water.

9. How to bring water where you need it, and to get rid of waste from where you don't want it.

10. How you will regulate internal and external temperature without heating and cooling equipment.

11. How vulnerable you will be in the absence of emergency services and the police, and what you may need to do to protect yourself and your family in the aftermath of a disaster

If you're not ready to *pull the plug* and rough it, don't feel bad, many people aren't. If 24 hours is too long, try the experiment for a shorter period of time, maybe a few hours. Here in Florida we have had many storms that have left entire communities without power for days; a few times for well over a week. For those folks who were prepared, the loss of power was manageable. For the unprepared, the loss of power was a major nightmare.

Being prepared and knowing what you might expect after any crisis, could give you an important advantage and allow you, and your family, to make the transition to *survival mode* quickly and effectively, and more importantly without fear or panic.

If all this is new to you, even the thought of preparing for any such event can seem overwhelming. It is best to start slowly, and to break it all down into manageable steps.

Here are some basic ideas and suggestions to help you get started.

• Make your first goal obtaining at least a 6-8 week supply of food, water, and first aid/medical supplies. (See the lists of suggested supplies). You will soon learn that if you have supplies, you don't need to go out looking for any, and you don't need to compete with other people who may be looking for the same things.

- Have a family security and self-defense plan, get proper training, and stock-up on all the essentials. Make sure everybody knows and understands the plan, and their role within the group.
- Plan to have at least three sources of alternative power, and the appropriate fuels, that can be stored and moved safely.
- Assess regional risks and plan for those events that are most likely to occur in your area – but don't make the mistake of completely dismissing other less likely events. Plan for those also, just devote more resources to the most likely occurrences first. For example hurricanes are very common in South Florida, earthquakes not so common. But, there is an obvious overlap in how you would prepare for both. In addition, just because something is not likely to happen where you live, doesn't mean it can't happen and that you shouldn't prepare for it.
- Plan for both bugging-in and bugging-out scenarios. (See All The Bugs, Chapter 7).
- Always have a Plan "B" and always have a back-up for everything you consider to be important. Remember, if you only have one, you have none.
- Keep it to yourself. Only your immediate family, and people in your group, should know about your plan and your preparations.
- Establish and maintain well-stocked first aid kits for common medical emergencies. Make sure that you and your group members know what supplies you have, and how to use them.

Plan on periodically reassessing and adjusting your plan as needs or conditions change. You can do the 24 hour experiment at any time, or you can do parts of it. Think of it as an extended fire drill. Thinking about different scenarios and planning for them is always a good idea. It's even better if you can live the actual moment and get a first-hand assessment of how effective, or ineffective, your plan and preparations are in real-life.

11: Tools of the Trade–Do You Have What It Takes?

Have you ever started a *do it yourself* job at home or work, only to discover that you don't really have the right tools to get the job done properly? Depending on the availability and relative price of the tools you need, you may have decided to just make-due with what you had and not waste time, or money, buying a tool you might not use that often – after all, how hard could it be? After several hours of struggling to *make due* you realize that the right tool would have made the job so much easier and faster. Frustration sets in and you decide to walk away and continue the job once you have the right tools.

Under normal circumstances you can run down to a big box retailer, or hardware store, where you will probably find a big selection of tools. You choose the style, price level, and quality you want. If you are not in a big hurry, you can even go on-line and search the web for the best tool, at the very best price, and have it delivered to your front door within days of purchase.

After a WCS there will be a lot of work to do including clean-up and repairs; you'll need the right tools to get those jobs done safely and effectively.

Here are some common overlooked situations:
- Clearing a yard of fallen trees after a storm.
- Digging through rubble after an earth quake.
- Repairing or securing the structures on your property.
- Patching up and re-enforcing an unsafe situation.
- Accessing and turning off water and gas line mains.

The list goes on and on. In a survival scenario, that little tool box, the one filled with small, cheaply made tools that is buried somewhere in your closet, will be of little or no value to you. In the coming days, months and maybe even longer, you will need tools; and you won't be able to run out and buy them.

This is one of those expenses that people struggle with since it requires an immediate outlay of cash for something you might put away and not use for a long time, or maybe never at all. But if you should ever need them, not having the right tools will cost you dearly.

I'll give you an example - in 1992 Hurricane Andrew destroyed many South Florida neighborhoods. After the storm many residents found themselves buried by fallen trees and large branches that were blocking roads, driveways, and the entrances to many homes. This was definitely a job for a chainsaw. But, most people didn't have a chainsaw. Overnight many enterprising people set-up shop on the side of major roads selling generators, chainsaws, and other tools, but they were selling these products at a 500% mark-up, and only for cash. Many people either could not, or would not, pay these prices, or had no cash since the power was out, and all the ATMs were either destroyed during the storm, without power, or had been completely depleted in the hours before the storm hit.

After Andrew I waited for a good sale and bought a chain saw. That was in 1992, as of today I have never had an occasion to use it. But I now have one along with fuel, oil, an extra chain and spare parts.

A word of caution – when you purchase survival tools, don't lend them to anyone. And I mean no one, it's that simple. We all have friends, neighbors and relatives who love to borrow tools and never return them, or worse yet, always return them broken or missing parts. Having your survival tools sitting somewhere in your friend's house will not help you in the aftermath of a crisis. Don't get me wrong, I am never opposed to helping a person in need, but your first obligation is to yourself and your family. These tools may one day help to save your life. Do you really want to wait until after a WCS to remember that your survival tools are in uncle Joe's garage buried somewhere under his holiday decorations.

Also, this is not a good time to be cheap. In life you usually get what you pay for. There is a big difference between buying quality at sale prices, and buying cheap stuff. There is a reason one shovel costs twenty dollars and another costs twice as much. Saving a few bucks may seem like a good deal until you go to use the tool and it breaks leaving you stranded. After a WCS is not the best time to find out that the cheaper tool was actually cheaper for a reason. That brings me to the next point - don't buy tools only to bring them home and put them away. You need to use those tools and become familiar with their strengths and weaknesses. Some may not be as effective, or durable, as you might have thought. If a tool is going to fail, have it fail now and not during a WCS. Buy the best tools you can afford, and then put them to the test. I am still using tools that I bought during the 1980s. I have taken care of them, and they have taken care of me.

I have put together a list of tools that I highly recommend you acquire. Remember, these are most of the tools I would want to have available to me during and after a disaster. In an ideal situation, I would even want to have more than one, since tools fail, break, don't function and very often just manage to get lost just when you need them the most. Also, every situation is different and the tools will vary accordingly. Someone living in an apartment in the city will not buy the same tools as someone living in a house in the suburbs.

The list is not in order of priority since every situation is different, but I have tried to list the most used and most commonly needed tools. What you eventually buy, will be determined by your budget, where you live, and what your needs are.

Tools For Before and After a WCS

- **Axe** – If possible get a few different sizes, and have back-ups. Axes literally take a pounding. Axe heads are un-likely to break, but handles, especially wood handles, break often. Store spare handles, or if you can afford it get the more expensive, and more durable, fiberglass handles. This advice applies to most, if not all, of the tools with handles.

- **Shovel(s)** – Have various sizes of long handled shovels. Have at least three digging shovels with strong padded handles, and at least two flat edged shovels. Also invest in at least two high quality short handle shovels.

- **Pickaxe** – Everything that applies to an axe, applies to a pickaxe. The large momentum of a heavy pickaxe can put a lot of effective power in your hands. Long handles are best for the heavy duty work, but a smaller, lighter short handle pickaxe will also come in handy in many situations, especially in tight quarters. The pickaxe has been used since prehistoric times for tasks ranging from farming to warfare. Have at least two.

- **Sledge Hammer** – Buy a few standard size sledge hammers, and invest at least one of the smaller one-handed models for those situations where a standard hammer is not heavy enough to get the job done.

- **Hammer** – For survival purposes look for full sized standard hammers for multiple purposes. The hammer may be the oldest tool known to exist there is a reason for this. Have at least three different size hammers.

- **Bolt Cutters** – Full size cutters and a smaller more manageable set will usually take care of most situations.

- **Pry Bars** – You should have at least one large, one medium and one small. Extras are always welcomed. I have broken small pry bars, and bent some of the larger ones. Get the best you can afford, and have no less than two.

- **Hand Saw** – Have various sizes with lots of spare blades. Have a selection of spare blades for cutting different materials, (i.e., wood, metal and plastic).

- **Chain Saw** – Have a good quality chain saw, with enough fuel, oil, spare chain and extra parts. A chain saw requires no electricity and can do a tremendous amount of work in very short order. This is what some might call a force multiplier tool, since one person can do the work of many with just one tool. *Make sure to always follow the manufacturer's instructions and to use eye and ear protection.*

- **Hard Hats, Eye & Ear Protection, Dust Masks, and Heavy Work Gloves.** These items are technically not tools, but they protect you when you are using tools and doing the *heavy lifting.* Remember there may be lots to do to get you *back on your feet* after a WCS, if you are fortunate enough to have people come to help it's up to you to make sure they are well equipped – have enough for all your people. Also these activities are inherently dangerous, without the proper safety equipment people can get seriously hurt – you should not take any unnecessary risks.

- **Machete** – This large, cleaver-like tool is lightweight, yet has enough blade weight to make it a very effective and durable cutting tool. The machete has been used successfully for years as an agricultural cutting tool, and as a weapon. There are many variations, pick the ones that suit you, and your needs best. Machetes are relatively inexpensive, buy at least two.

- **Gas/Water Shut Off Tool** – These are inexpensive, but come in very handy. Buy a few and keep them readily visible and available for an emergency.

- **Power Drill with Extra Batteries** – Buy a high quality 18 volt power drill with at least two extra batteries, (Lithium-Ion). Keep charged at all times and rotate the batteries.

- **Socket & Ratchet Set** – Have a high quality socket and ratchet set with attachments, extensions and a complete variety of SAE and metric-sized sockets. Look for American made high quality steel tools; spend a little extra money here.

- **Wheel Barrel** – A wheel barrel outfitted with solid, puncture proof tires can help save you hours of back breaking work. Have at least one, more if you have a large property.

- **Hand Truck** – A personal hand truck is a great item for moving heavy objects quickly and efficiently. Or if you need to carry several stacked boxes that aren't easily carried by hand. Some models fold up when nor in use. Get one that is sturdy and well built.

- **Gas Powered Portable Generator** – A gas generator can be a real life-saver when there's a power outage. Try to pick a size that works for you and your needs. I prefer the name brand engines (Briggs & Stratton and Honda for example) with a pull start versus a battery start. Batteries must be maintained on a charger to avoid a dead battery. A pull start doesn't rely on a battery and is more dependable – mine has always started on the first pull. (Don't forget to have several heavy duty extension cords.)

- **Portable Heating And Air Conditioning Units** – Depending on where you live, and the time of year a crisis erupts, you may need to regulate the temperature inside your home. There are many portable heating and cooling units on the market that operate on back-up generator power or on other fuels. Depending on your needs, make sure to secure the necessary equipment well in advance of any crisis, to test it and to keep it in good working order for when the need arises.

- **Fire Extinguishers** – High quality fire extinguishers, placed throughout the house, are a must.

Ways to Save Money

- Buy used tools. Visit garage, estate sales and second hand shops. You would be surprised by what you can sometimes get for just a few dollars.

- Look for sales at local retailers and on-line. Look for coupons and special sales, free shipping or other perks that lower the overall price.

- Tool of the month club. Buy one or more tools each month. By the end of the year you will have a lot more than you have now.

- Cooperate with neighbors. Coordination with your neighbors will save you money. Make sure, however, that you neighbors are as committed to the effort as you are. During a WCS is no time to find out that your neighbor let his cousin's best friend borrow the chain saw and he never got it back.

- Buy quality tools. Cheap tools will not last long. Having to replace tools often will be more expensive than if you had just purchased a quality tool to begin with. Cheap tools are also more dangerous to use, since tool failures can often cause serious injuries to the user. During a WCS, a tool failure, especially one resulting in an injury, can really mess up your day.

Depending on your needs, and your budget, make sure to secure the best possible tools available. If you live in a small apartment, or are otherwise limited by storage space, make the most of what you have. Fewer tools will mean that you'll need to be more selective. Don't wait until the last minute to start assessing your requirements and acquiring your tools.

12: Shopping Lists–What You'll Need

Shopping for survival gear and supplies can be fun, but it can also be a daunting task. What to buy, how much to buy, what to store, how to store it? For many people just trying to put together a list can be an overwhelming task. As you start assessing your needs you'll realize that there are a long list of things that you should be stocking, but probably aren't. Some of these items may not be essential for survival, but everything on the list(s) will make your life easier in a disaster situation, especially in a Bugging-In scenario. During times of high stress, anything that can bring a little "normal" back into your life, and make you feel better is worth having. Some of these items may not be relevant to you, if so, pick the ones that are and start your own list. The idea here is to give you a starting point from which you can begin and customize your own list. Our list is not in order of importance, but is organized by category – some items may overlap.

Supplies That Every Home Should Have

Water - Storage & Disinfection
- Emergency Supply of Bottled Water (One Gallon Bottles and Smaller)
- Five to Seven Gallon BPA Free Reusable Water Containers with Spigot
- Manual Water Pump(s)
- Drinking Water Safe Hose
- 5 Gallon Food Safe Buckets, with Lids
- Funnels (Plastic) - Different Sizes
- Chlorine Bleach (Unscented)
- Tincture of Iodine 2% and Povidone - Iodine Solution 10%
- High Capacity Water Filter with Extra Filter Elements

- Lightweight, Potable Water Filter For When You're on-the-Move
- Coffee Filters for Pre-Filtering Dirty Water
- Eye droppers (At least Half a Dozen)

Food & Food Storage

- Ready to Eat Canned Foods – Meats, Beans, Fruits, Vegetables, Soups, and Stews
- Canned Tuna, Sardines, Salmon, Chicken and Pork Products
- Peanut Butter – Smooth or Crunchy
- Rolled Oats – Instant or Original
- White Rice – Instant and Regular
- Uncooked Beans – Black, Red, Navy, Lentils, Split Pea
- Canned Beans - Black, Red, Navy, Lentils, Split Pea
- Milk – Powdered, Sweetened Condensed, and Evaporated
- Manual/Hand-Can Openers
- Salt – Sea Salt and Regular
- Pepper - Pre-ground and Whole Pepper Corns
- Variety of Dried Spices – Garlic, Onions, Oregano, & Italian Seasoning
- Vanilla Extract
- Soy Sauce, Ketchup and BBQ Sauce
- Chicken, Beef and Vegetable Stock
- Bouillon Cubes, Pre-Made or Powered Gravy
- Honey and Maple Syrup
- White and Brown Sugar
- Corn Starch
- Flour and Yeast
- Baking Soda
- Baking Powder
- Cooking Oil – Vegetable and Canola
- Cooking Spray
- Olive Oil

- Vinegar
- Manual Grain Grinder
- Liquor/Alcohol
- Energy Bars, Granola, Crackers, Chips, Nuts, Candies and Gum
- Coffee, Teas and Filters
- Chocolate Syrup
- Powdered Water Enhancers – Different Flavors
- Powdered Ice Tea Mix
- A Case of Assorted Meals, Ready-to-Eat (MREs)
- Aluminum Foil (Regular and Heavy Duty)
- Storage/Freezer Bags – Sandwich, Quart and Gallon Sizes
- Five gallon Pails with Covers/Lids - Long-Term Food Storage
- Removable Air-Tight Sealed Lids that Unscrew Off (They Come In Different Colors to Help Identify Contents)
- Oxygen Absorbers (2000cc) –Long-Term Food Storage
- Five Gallon Mylar Bags - Long-Term Food Storage

First Aid & Medical
- C-A-T Combat Application Tourniquet
- Celox First Aid Traumatic Wound Treatment
- Celox V12090 – Blood Clotting Granule Applicator and Plunger Set
- Chest Seal – For The Management of Penetrating Chest Wounds
- Gauze Pads – (4X4-inch) Larges Pads
- Triangular Bandages
- Multi-Purpose Bandages
- Tactical Trauma Dressing, Israeli Bandages
- Steri-Strip Wound Closure Strips
- Tegaderm Transparent Film
- Nitrile Exam Gloves (Different Sizes)

- Adhesive Bandages (Different Sizes)
- First Aid Tape – Plain Waterproof in Various Sizes.
- Elastic Bandage 3"
- Triple Antibiotic Ointment
- Burn Gel - First Aid Burn Treatment
- Povidone-Iodine 10%
- Alcohol Prep Pads
- CPR Face Shield
- Ibuprofen
- Acetaminophen
- Aspirin
- Instant Cold Compress
- Prescription Strength Pain Relievers
- Broad Spectrum Antibiotics
- Tempa-Dot Disposable Thermometers
- Electronic Children's Thermometer
- Old Fashioned Glass Thermometer
- Nuun Portable Electrolyte Hydration
- Small LED Flashlight
- Hands-Free Headlamp
- Shears, Bandage Scissors
- IV Fluids and Needles (Different Sizes)
- Sutures (Different Sizes)
- Needle Holders, Suture Scissors and Forceps
- Epinephrine Injection
- Blood Pressure Set
- Resuscitation Bag
- Eye Pads
- Eye Wash
- Activated Charcoal
- Moleskin
- Berman Oral Airway Kit
- Stay Alert Gum
- Aluminum Splint

Personal Hygiene & Cleanliness

- Soap – Bars and Liquid
- Anti-Bacterial Soap
- Toothpaste and Toothbrushes
- Floss - Waxed & Un-Waxed
- Mouthwash and Fluoride Rinse
- Shampoo
- Lice Shampoo
- Deodorant
- Razor Blades, Shaving Cream
- Body Lotion – Unscented or Lightly Scented
- Q-tips, Cotton Balls
- Toilet Paper
- Pre-Moistened Wipes
- Feminine Napkins
- Feminine Hygiene Products
- Anti-Bacterial Wipes
- Disinfecting Sprays
- Antibacterial Gels and Lotions
- Condoms

Health and Wellness

- Prescription Medications – Minimum of Three Month Supply
- Antibiotics – Wide Selection (See First Aid Supplies List in Chapter 5)
- Vitamins – Store the Ones You Normally Take
- Eye drops and Eye Wash
- Isopropyl (rubbing) Alcohol
- Alcohol Wipes
- Hydrogen Peroxide
- Glasses – Prescription and for Sun Protection
- Antacid Tablets or Liquid
- Anti-Diarrhea Tablets

- Sunscreen, Aloe Lotion or Gel, and Bug spray
- Birth control – (Prescriptions and Condoms)

Clothes and Comfort
- Extra Pants, Shirts, Underwear, Socks
- Thermal Underwear
- Selection of Varied Outerwear for Seasons
- Cold Weather Gloves
- Comfortable Walking Shoes and Boots
- Rain Gear, Waterproof Boots and/or Rubber Boots
- Waterproof Gloves
- Waterproof Poncho
- Hats for Sun, Rain and Cold
- Sleeping Bags,
- Blankets and Pillows
- Backpack
- Sunglasses, Clear lens Safety Glasses for Eye Protection

Household Goods and Safety
- Selection of Household Cleaning Supplies
- Laundry Detergent
- Chlorine Bleach (Unscented)
- Wash Board and Clothes Pins (for Laundry)
- Sponges, Towels and Wash clothes
- Paper Plates (Various Sizes)
- Paper/Plastic Cups (Various Sizes)
- Plastic Utensils (Forks, Spoons, Knives)
- Paper Towels, Napkins
- Garbage Bags (All Sizes)
- Sewing Supplies, Scissors, Fabrics, Zippers, Buttons, Patches, Velcro
- Paper and Pencils
- Mop and Bucket with Wringer
- Fire Extinguishers – Placed Throughout the House

- Mouse and Rat Traps
- Non-Toxic Ant and Cockroach Traps
- Rat Poison for Extreme Infestations
- Ant, Wasp, Hornet and Roach Sprays

For the Kids

- Baby and Toddler Supplies – Diapers, Wipes, Soap, Lotion, Baby Powder
- Children's Thermometer
- Fever Reducer (acetaminophen), Cold Medicine, Diarrhea Medicine
- Commercially available Therapeutic Hydration Fluids to Prevent Dehydration
- Extra Prescription Medications and Copies of Prescriptions
- Children's Toothbrush, Toothpaste and Mouth Rinse
- Children's Clothes and Shoes – Variety for Seasons and Sizes
- Books, Games and Other Materials to Entertain and Pass the Time
- Favorite Stuffed Animal or Toys
- Flashlights – Small Plastic Flashlights
- Non-Perishable Small Snacks or Finger Foods

Tools and General Outdoor

- Portable Generator –Minimum 3000 Watts
- Basic Hand Tools – Hammer, Screwdrivers, Pliers, Utility Knife
- Garden Tools – Shovels, Pick Axe, Axe, Wedge
- Work Gloves – At Least 5 Pairs
- Knives and Sharpening Tools
- Files – An Assortment of Sizes
- Hand Saw with Extra Blades
- Bow Saw, with Extra Blades
- Chain Saw, Extra Parts, Gasoline and Oil
- Gasoline Containers – As many as Possible

- Gas Stabilizer
- Engine/Motor Oil
- Engine Starting Fluid
- Extra Spark Plugs, Air filters
- Manual Tire and Air Pump
- Lubricating, Moisture Displacing and Silicone Spray
- Bolts, Nails Screws, Washers - Large Assortment of Different Types/Sizes
- Duct Tape, Electrical Tape
- 550 Para Cord, Rope, Tie Wraps, Bungee Cords and Straps
- Assortment of Different Glues/Adhesives
- Spare Parts for Any and All Gear, Tools and Equipment
- 5 Gallon Buckets, Lids
- Flashlights and Lanterns
- Fuel and Extra Wicks for Lanterns
- Extra Batteries – Large Assortment of Types and Sizes
- Fertilizers
- Pest Control Sprays and Powders
- Charcoal/Lighter Fluid
- Waterproof and Strike Anywhere Matches
- Selection of Disposable and Refillable Lighters with Extra Lighter Fluid
- Alternate Fire Starters
  o   Magnesium Fire Stick
  o   Swedish Fire Steel
  o   Magnifying Glass
- Gun Cleaning Supplies
- Camp Stove and Extra Fuel
- Propane Cook Top – Outdoor
- Outdoor Cookware
- Portable Toilets
- Propane Tanks – 20 LB Standard Tank & 16.4 oz Disposable Mini
- Mini Water Heater with Extra Fuel

- Lumber – Assortment of Various Sizes and Cuts
- Plywood Panels
- Rolls of Plastic Sheeting (10ft. X 25ft. no less than 6mil)
- Plastic Tarps – Various Sizes
- Patches for Tarps
- Coolers (Various Sizes with Locking Lids)
- Manual Fuel/Water Pump
- Spray Paint in Various Colors
- Eye, Ear and Face Protection – Have Extra Sets
- Chains – Various Thickness and Lengths
- Pad Locks and Several Lengths of Heavy Chain
- Mouse Traps – Different Sizes
- Charcoal and Lighter Fluid
- Fire Extinguishers
- Plastic Garbage Cans
- Wagon, Hand Truck and Spare Tires
- Bicycles with Extra Parts, Tires, Inner Tubes, and Hand Air Pump
- Portable Space Heater
- Portable Air Conditioning Unit

Self-Defense and Personal Protection

- Firearms
  - 12 Gauge Shotgun
  - AR-15/M4 Style Rifle in 5.56/.223
  - Compact Semi-Automatic Pistol in No Less Than 9mm
- Ammunition
  - 12 Gauge Shotgun Shells (00 Buck Shot, Bird Shot and Slugs) – Minimum 500-750 Shells
  - 5.56/.223, Full Metal Jacket for Practice; and Self-Defensive Rounds - Minimum 3000 Rounds
  - 9mm, Full Metal Jacket for Practice; and Self-Defensive Rounds - Minimum 5000 Rounds

- Collapsible Baton
- Pepper Spray
- Handcuffs, Ties
- Accessories for Firearms – Extra Magazines, Optics, Night Sights Slings, Holsters, Flashlights, Lasers, etc.
- Cleaning Kits and Extra Cleaning Supplies
- Spare Parts for All Firearms
- Body Armor and Ballistics Vest
- Eye and Ear Protection – Have Extra Sets
- Gloves, Knee and Elbow Pads

Information/Reference Materials

- Survival Books and Magazines
- Medical/First Aid Reference Materials and Books, Outdoor Emergency Medicine
- Trauma First Aid Books
- Writing Paper, Pens, Pencils, Solar Calculator
- Waterproof Plastic Sleeve for Copies of All Important Personal Documents
- Waterproof Plastic Sleeve to Keep Local and Regional Maps
- Waterproof Plastic Sleeve for Copies of All Insurance Policies
- Waterproof Plastic Sleeve for Copies of All Legal Documents
- Owner's Manuals and Operating Guides for all Tools, Equipment and Mechanical Devices.

Appendix A: Same Day, Two Very Different Lives

Complacency: Defined as a real state of mind, where one is both unaware and inappropriately comfortable in the presence of hazards.

The Unprepared

Day 1

You get up one morning, and naturally go about your daily routine; having breakfast, getting dressed and preparing for the day ahead. The phone rings and it's your friend from work, asking if you have heard the news yet. You turn on the television to find that every single channel is carrying the same story. Apparently some obscure terrorist group is taking credit for a series of overnight cyber attacks. These coordinated attacks were carried out against utilities, and other high value targets, including computer networks throughout the U.S. and around the world. These cyber incursions have had a devastating effect on the electrical grid and other vital national resources. Government officials are reading prepared statements, asking people to remain calm, and trying to reassure the public that everything is under control. The feigned official calm and confidence seems to be having the opposite effect; news stations from around the country report that people have already started panic buying of gasoline, food, water and other essentials. "And by the way" your friend says, "the office is closed today – we have a day off! Isn't that awesome?"

You decide to drive to your local gas station to fill your gas tank; just in case. Maybe you'll pick up a few gallons of water, bread and perhaps some canned goods and a flashlight – better to do it now before things get worse. You're sure that the government, FEMA and local authorities will quickly address the problems and get things back to normal, but you would feel a whole lot better with a full tank of gas and some extra supplies around the house. Traffic is unusually heavy even for rush hour. A drive that normally takes five to ten minutes takes you forty-five minutes. You arrive at the gas station to find the attendants walking around with handwritten cardboard signs that say "NO MORE GAS, DELIVERY EXPECTED TOMORROW". A number of people, who had been waiting on the non-moving line, angrily walk up to the station only to get the bad news. A few people start arguing with the station manager – the situation is getting pretty ugly.

Less than two blocks down the road, the local grocery store is in no better shape. An older lady, who is standing outside the store banging on the glass doors with a clenched fist, says that the store manager just locked the doors after some people started fighting over the last items on the shelves. In less than a few hours after the news broke, the store shelves were stripped completely bare.

A few minutes after you arrive, the lights start to flicker; finally going completely dark. As you walk away, you see a store employee taping a sign to the inside of the glass door that says that the store is closed until further notice.

You head back home empty-handed and shaken by how quickly things have gone from "normal" to *every-man-for-himself.* On the drive home you see a number of accidents. Emergency vehicles, with lights flashing and sirens blaring, are fighting to get through the congestion. On the car radio, you start hearing more details about the attacks. According to the news anchor the terrorists seem to have targeted the electrical grid and the computers and networks that manage the nation's power systems; and the all-important movement of electricity between utilities and their clients. In the early morning hours, a massive number of strategically planned cyber attacks had overwhelmed a relatively small but critically important network of computers that manage a significant segment of the distribution of electricity over the grid.

On another radio station the commentator is interviewing a terrorism expert. The expert is saying that the terrorist had finally found the mother of all *Achilles' heel* – our dependence on electrical power. From the basics, like water, food and temperature control to our reliance on computers and the internet for everything from banking to getting our prescriptions filled. Without ever having set foot on American soil, the hackers were taking us apart one piece at a time; complete social and economic disruption on a massive scale.

As it turned out, this was not a typical isolated power outage, or a localized storm, or even a bomb attack on a specific target. This was widespread pandemonium on a scale that the US population had never seen before, and it was spreading wider with every passing moment. There was a deafening silence that followed his remarks. This particular news anchor, who always managed to make a big deal out of small and inconsequential local stories, was at a loss for words. The expert continued with his theory..."After 9/11 many terrorist organizations realized that even large scale coordinate attacks, such as the ones on 9/11, would not produce the kind of disruption and destruction that the terrorist were looking to achieve. In a series of smaller, less detectable attacks, hackers had probed our networks looking for opportunities." It was not yet entirely known how it all came about, but the commentator surmised that the terrorist had somehow used botnets in the attacks. A botnet – short for "robot networks" could have allowed the terrorist to command unknown numbers of computers using spyware, worms, or viruses which would have been previously introduced through the internet connections. With a single command, originating from anywhere in the world, the botnet master could instruct each of the many slave computers to contact any number of networks causing such high demand on its ports as to bring it all crashing down.

When a target is compromised, the attackers move on to the next – bring down enough targets and you start a domino effect. If the target is a utility company, hospital, police/fire department or any network that the public relies on, the attacks can seriously jeopardize public health and safety. But this is exactly what the terrorist wanted – to cause fear, panic and as much social disruption as possible. They knew that stripping away that very thin veneer that most of us confuse with civilized behavior would be relatively easy once the basic social infra-structure was disrupted.

For years many security officials and non-partisan organizations had issued warnings amid ever growing concerns that the U.S. was not adequately prepared for a major cyber attack. But, even as hack-ers, criminal organizations, and foreign governments continued to probe and infiltrate critical networks, efforts to improve cyber secu-rity stalled in the House and Senate. The *business-as-usual* politicians pointed fingers, blamed each other, and made a lot of accusations, but did nothing more. In the end, none of it mattered much – in reality we the people were to blame. For years voters sent ineffective leaders to Washington, and then complained that government was ineffec-tive. Go figure.

One thing was painfully clear; the terrorist had somehow found and exploited a very serious weakness. The attacks were literally mov-ing at the speed of light shutting down large portions of the grid.

The portions of the grid that still remained viable after the attacks were quickly overwhelmed by the extraordinary demand and also began to fail. In an effort to prevent further damage to the grid and to re-route the remaining electricity to police, fire departments, hospitals and essential government services, officials disabled large seg-ments of the grid redirected power to key sections.

Arriving home you greet a few neighbors that are standing around outside; one guy thinks it's a government plot; another person is ram-bling on about judgment day and the rapture. Rather than listening to anymore nonsense you go inside to take a quick inventory of your supplies. You have a few cans of tuna, some pasta, a bag of instant rice, some canned tomatoes, a box of cereal, a bottle of soda and a few cans of fruit juice. You also find an old radio that runs on batteries, a flashlight that has seen better days, a few scented candles and about five small bottles of water – not great, but better than nothing. You had always wanted to stock-up on food, water and emergency supplies but somehow never got around to doing it. There was never enough time, and money was always in short supply.

You remember reading an article about urban survival and how the author had recommended keeping no less than two gallons per person, per day of water for drinking, at least one month supply of canned goods, medical supplies, prescriptions, and many other things you can't even remember. It always seemed so expensive, and felt foolish to buy and stock up on things that you did not need at that moment. And what were the odds that anything would actually happen that would not get resolved within a few days? In retrospect you wish that maybe you had put more time and effort into research, planning, and preparation.

You still have power, but the lights keep dimming and flickering. By early evening the power finally goes out and stays out. On the radio the announcer says that the station is operating on back-up generators and that they will continue transmitting for as long as possible.

Once darkness arrives the neighborhood is filled with an eerie quiet. A few homes are running back-up generators, and others have camping style lights, but most homes are dark. Down the block a few families are throwing a "Grid-Down" party and drinking what seemed like an endless supply of beer, that they keep pulling out of a blue and white cooler. Finally, they run out of beer, or maybe just grow tired and they called it a night - thank goodness. You lay down on the sofa for what seemed hours; it's amazing all the sounds that you can hear when the windows are open and the all too familiar hum of electrical appliances goes silent. A strange fear grabs you as you consider that this situation may not get resolved anytime soon.

Day 7

A week later the power is still out, and the water has stopped flowing from the tap. Luckily, a few days before, one of your neighbors had suggested that you start filling all empty containers with water just in case. A few people were outside today trying to fill some buckets from a fire hydrant.

You want to go outside to talk to some of your neighbors to see if anyone has heard anything, but a few nights ago you almost got caught in the middle of a very nasty argument that ended in a savage fight between two men. Instead of coming together to try and figure this out and help each other, the hostility among neighbors was actually intensifying. Starting that day you stayed inside as much as possible.

Day 12

In the weeks that followed, a group of thugs had started coming around scavenging for food, water or anything they could carry away. There had been no parties on your block since that first night. Your food and water is running dangerously low, but you don't dare go outside.

Day 21

Three weeks into the nightmare you are almost completely out of food and water and you're starting to panic. But you dare not go outside. The day before yesterday a neighbor told you that there are rumors that the government is imposing a dusk to dawn curfew to reestablish order in the major cities and surrounding communities. Throughout the night you can hear the sounds of gunshots, sirens and screaming. Late last night you woke up to the sounds of gun fire and what sounded like someone kicking in a door. After that it all went quiet. You are very scared and panic is starting to set in.

The Prepared

Imagine the very same nightmare scenario, but this time the person in our story was prepared.

As soon as you started seeing the early warning signs you kick start your emergency plan. You, your family, and your support group are all on the same page. You have a predetermined place to meet, a way to communicate and to look for each other if the need arises. Each of you has a BOB, a GHB and a good stash of emergency food, water, medical/first aid supplies, cash and extra fuel. You have also taken steps to ensure the safety and security of yourself and your loved ones – you have adequate supplies of guns, ammunition, and body armor. It is not entirely clear in the initial days of the crisis if you will bug-in or out, but you are prepared and have a plan for either eventuality. You are concerned and apprehensive but you're not panicking.

The Story Continues…

_____

Share your thoughts with others - please take a moment to review *Surviving Doomsday* on Amazon.com

"Stay Safe and Be Prepared!"
Richard Duarte

Appendix B: Glossary

ACP: Automatic Colt pistol.

AR-15: A lightweight, magazine fed, semi-automatic rifle.

BOB: Bug-out bag. A portable kit that contains the essentials required for survival for a short period of time. The primary purpose of a BOB is to allow a person to evacuate quickly if a crisis strikes.

BPA: Bisphenol A. BPA is an industrial chemical that has been used to make certain plastics since the 1960s.

Black Friday: The day following Thanksgiving in the U.S. On this day retailers open their doors extremely early and lower their prices to attract early holiday shoppers.

Bug-Back: Getting back home after some major disaster occurs while you are away from home.

Bug-In: The opposite of Bugging out; the act of sheltering in place.

Bug-Out: The act of removing yourself from one location to another very quickly; usually at the because of some crisis or a natural or manmade disaster.

CDC: Centers for Disease Control. A U.S. federal agency under the department of Health and Human Services, tasked with protecting human health and safety.

CPR: Cardiopulmonary resuscitation. An emergency procedure used to keep the heart pumping and oxygen flowing until emergency care arrives.

CQB: Close Quarter Battle. A type of fighting in which the enemy is engage using small arms in confined spaces using military tactics.

CQC: Close Quarter Combat. A type of fighting in which the enemy is engage using small arms in confined spaces using military tactics.

EMS: Emergency medical services.

FDA: Food and Drug Administration. The FDA is a federal government agency responsible for protecting and regulating public health.

FEMA: Federal Emergency Management Agency. FEMA is a federal government agency responsible for coordinating disaster relief.

GHB: Get home bag. Similar in concept to a bug-out bag, but intended to contain items and supplies to help you get home, from some other location, after a major crisis.

Glock: Widely used line of polymer-framed semi-automatic pistols.

IV Fluids: Intravenous therapy or IV therapy is the giving of liquid substances directly into a vein.

M4: The M4 carbine is a select-fire, shorter and lighter variant of the M16 assault rifle.

MRE: Meals, Ready to Eat. Self-contained, individual field rations used by the military.

NATO: North Atlantic Treaty Organization.

PET: Polyethylene terephthalate. A polymer resin used to make beverage and food safe containers.

SAFE ROOM: A safe room or panic room is a fortified room which is installed in a private residence to provide a safe hiding place for the occupants.

SODIS: Short for solar water disinfection. SODIS is a method of disinfecting water using only sunlight, and plastic PET bottles.

WCS: Worst Case Scenario.

Appendix C: Recommended Books

- **HAWKE'S GREEN BERET SURVIVAL GUIDE – BY: MYKEL HAWKE**
  (No-nonsense, straight forward survival guide; easy to read and follow. One of best survival books available; and one on my favorites)

- **WHEN ALL HELL BREAKS LOOSE – BY: CODY LUNDIN**
  (Very good reference material, lots of excellent information presented in a very entertaining fashion as only Cody Lundin can.)

- **98.6 DEGREES – THE ART OF KEEPING YOUR ASS ALIVE – BY: CODY LUNDIN**
  (Very Practical and useful material, again presented as only Cody Lundin can.)

- **HOW TO SURVIVE THE END OF THE WORLD AS WE KNOW IT – BY: JAMES W. RAWLES**
  (Tactics, techniques and technologies for uncertain times – need we say more? Well written and very informative.)

- **U.S. ARMED FORCES SURVIVAL GUIDE – BY: JOHN BOSWELL**
  (Good reference survival guide).

- **WILDERNESS SURVIVAL – BY: GREGORY J. DAVENPORT**
  (Good reference survival guide).

- **MEDICINE FOR THE OUTDOORS – BY: PAUL S. AUERBACH, MD**
(No-nonsense, straight forward medical survival guide; easy to read and understand. One of best first aid survival books available. Handy lists of supplies needed for a comprehensive first aid kit).

- **ENCYCLOPEDIA OF COUNTRY LIVING – BY: CARLA EMERY**
(Essential, one-of-a-kind, encyclopedia for living off-the-grid. Handy reference guide for just about anything you will ever want to know. One of the very best available resource of its kind)

- **SAS SURVIVAL HANDBOOK – POCKET EDITION- BY: JOHN WISEMAN**
(Pocket sized edition of the SAS – A-Z survival guide in a size that's perfect for your BOB).

About the Author

The first thing you should know about me is that I am obsessed with the topic of survival, especially urban survival. I don't know if technically it's an obsession, or a very strong passion, but I am definitely on a mission. I'm always ready to talk *survival* with anyone who will listen.

I don't live in an underground bunker, and I'm not preparing for a zombie apocalypse; well maybe I'm preparing a little, just in case. I have, however, survived some very scary events and have spent the last twenty years figuring out what works and what doesn't – often the hard way.

I'm a father of four, a grandfather, a husband and a responsible member of society that refuses to delegate my responsibility for my family's welfare to the government, or to anyone else for that matter. When I'm not writing, speaking, teaching or thinking about survival, I am busy practicing law and running my law office.

Read this book. And if it helps you, tell your friends and loved ones about it, and ask them to read it. There are no guarantees in life, but after any major disaster two separate and distinct groups will emerge - the prepared and the unprepared. It's up to you what group you'll belong to. As far as I'm concerned, the ultimate measure of this book's success will be how many people it can help guide into the *prepared group*.

For the latest news and updates, connect with Richard on
www.survivingdoomsdaythebook.com